Winning the
Timeshare Game:
Buying the Bargains

Winning the Timeshare Game: Buying the Bargains

How to Find the Deals,
Avoid the Scams, and Save Thousands

Written by Deanna Keahey
with success stories by Brian Cook

Winning the Timeshare Game: Buying the Bargains
How to Find the Deals, Avoid the Scams, and Save Thousands

Published in the United States by B&D Success Publishing

Portions of this book may also be incorporated in website and
training materials made available through
TimeshareGame.com.

First Edition

Library of Congress Cataloguing in Publication Data has been
applied for.

ISBN - 978-0-9888392-1-2

To Brian. Without your inspiration,
insights and unflagging support, this
book would not exist.

"Life is what we make it,
always has been, always will be."
~ Grandma Moses

Table of Contents

4. How YOU Want to Buy a Timeshare   53

5. Considerations When Buying a Timeshare   67

6. Finances of Buying a Timeshare   91

Acknowledgements and Credits   183

Introduction

Who needs this book?

This book is for you if...

* You like the concept of timeshares, but don't want to spend a fortune
* You'd like to take budget vacations with your family, spouse or friends
* You're wondering if a timeshare would be a good deal for you
* You're eyeing a timeshare, and want to make sure it's a smart buy
* **Saving ten thousand dollars** would totally make your day
* You're sick of people trying to take advantage of you
* You paid too much before, and don't want to make that mistake twice
* You want to learn how to **Win the Timeshare Game**

How to use this book

Where to start?

☐ You can start at the beginning of the book and read it straight through to the end.

☐ You can skip directly to the sections that fit your immediate needs, using the *Quick start guide*.

Terminology -- The timeshare industry has its own jargon that may be unfamiliar and confusing to those new to the field. If you're not sure about a certain term, consult the *Timeshare glossary* near the end of this book.

Notations used -- Throughout the book, you'll see these notations that mark important pieces of information:

Scam alerts -- These are common scams that are used to take advantage of people and get their money. Watch out for these and beware if you run into them in real life.

Insider tips -- These are expert tips from timeshare owners with years of experience. Taking advantage of these tips can save you money, time, and headaches.

Key questions -- These are important questions for you to think about. Your answers to these will make a difference in how to best proceed in the Timeshare Game.

Important notes

Research your own deals -- You need to do your own due diligence on every deal. Stories used in this book illustrate real life results that have been obtained, but do not guarantee the results of any other timeshare purchase. Your results could vary. Each timeshare deal has its own unique characteristics, and you need to thoroughly investigate your own opportunity before proceeding.

Changing rules -- The timeshare industry is known for changing the rules and introducing new twists. Everything in this book was researched and checked as of the publication date, but verify the rules on your own when you're investigating a deal. Every company has its own rules, and they keep changing.

Prices -- All prices in the book are quoted in US dollars, and are subject to change. Fees will vary in different countries (it's not necessarily a straight currency conversion), and prices could change at any time.

Legal advice -- The authors of this book are not lawyers, and this book does not offer any legal advice. If you have questions about the law or require legal counsel, consult an attorney familiar with timeshare law.

Quick start guide

If you want to skip straight to the sections that are most applicable to you, use this quick start guide. Determine your current position in the Timeshare Game, and find out what to read next.

Learning about timeshares

☐ **First thinking of it.** Your friends sometimes talk about timeshares, and you'd like to learn what this is all about. Start with *Timeshare fundamentals.*

☐ **Interested but confused**. You know something about timeshares, but all the different options and terminology get very complicated. See *Types of timeshare ownership.*

Going to a timeshare presentation

☐ **Attending a presentation soon. URGENT!** Read the following sections before you walk into that presentation:
How a typical presentation works,
Tactics they may use on you, and
Saying No, No, No to the hard sell.

☐ **Going to a presentation in 4+ hours**. You've got a little time to learn more before you meet the salesperson. Read the entire section *How THEY want you to buy a timeshare*, and follow the preparation steps recommended in *Skip the presentation, or use it for research.*

Interested in buying a timeshare bargain

☐ **Wondering where to start**. You like the idea of buying a discount timeshare, but you're not sure how to find the deals. Turn to *Where to find timeshare bargains.*

☐ **Not sure what to look for**. There are many things to think about before you purchase a timeshare. Start by reading the section *Considerations before you buy a timeshare.*

☐ **Thinking about finances**. A timeshare purchase involves both initial outlays and on-going financial obligations. If you want to understand the monetary aspects of timesharing, read *Finances of buying a timeshare.*

☐ **Narrowing the possibilities**. You've got one or more bargain timeshares you're looking at, and you're wondering how to find out which (if any) would be good to purchase. Look at *How to research a timeshare bargain.*

Already bought a timeshare

☐ **You've got buyer's remorse**. You just fell for the salesman's spiel, and signed up for an expensive timeshare. A couple of days later, you have buyer's remorse. **URGENT!** Read
Fall for the hard sell? You may have an out.

☐ **You're happy with your timeshare**. Many people who discover the wonderful world of timeshares end up buying a second or third. If you're an experienced buyer, the tips in this book can help you get an even better buy on your next one. Just skip to whatever section makes sense for you.

Once you're a timeshare owner, you'll also be interested in our companion book **Winning the Timeshare Game: Making the Most of Your Timeshare**, that gives you hundreds of tips and techniques to maximize your timeshare benefits.

1. Winning the Game: How Does it Work?

Timeshares - winning and losing

When you talk to people who have owned timeshares, you'll find they tend to split into two groups.

* One group owns timeshares (often more than one), and they get a lot of enjoyment from their timeshare vacations. They know how to work the system, avoid the scams, and find the deals. Knowing how to play the game successfully means they get bargain purchases, discount vacations, and stays at wonderful resorts. These people are **winning the timeshare game**.

* The other group has been ripped off and taken advantage of, and they think the entire timeshare industry is about scamming people and taking their money. They get more frustration from their timeshares than enjoyment, and they're unhappy with the entire system. Unfortunately, the bad experiences these people have had, cause them to miss out on the great benefits that are available. These people are **losing the game** - at least so far.

The difference between ending up in one group vs. the other often boils down to being an educated buyer who knows the ins and outs of timeshares. Those who walk into a timeshare presentation without the right knowledge will probably be taken advantage of. Those who know what they're doing can research their own deals, make smart decisions, and wind up a winner.

This book is here to give you the information you need - the inside secrets the resorts don't want you to know. If you learn these tips and techniques before your next foray into the timeshare market, **you can be one of the timeshare winners, too**.

Losing story
Spend $105,000 and pay for years

Couple A got an invitation for a free 3-day vacation, if they attended a timeshare presentation in California. After touring the resort, they sat down with a timeshare salesman.

He told them the perfect plan for them was a 2-bedroom timeshare that sold for $65,000, but was on an incredible sale for $45,000 that day only. They didn't have the cash, so he said he could work out affordable financing.

The quick and easy resort tour they were expecting turned into an ordeal that lasted over 5 hours. The pressure was high, and eventually they succumbed. The interest on the financing brought the total cost of their timeshare to $105,000 payable over 15 years ($7,000/year).

That's not all. Add in the annual fees of $1,295, and they owe $8,295 per year. That's a heavy financial burden for a young couple, when they could be saving for a home instead. Worst of all, they can't sell it for anything near the purchase price, so even if they sold, they'd still be underwater on the financing.

Winning story
Spend $1 and save for years

Couple B love to vacation in Florida, and go there every year. After numerous visits, they've gotten a feel for some of the resorts in the area, and thought they'd like to buy a timeshare there.

Knowing some resorts they'd be interested in owning, they started searching online and watching for a deal. After a few weeks, they found a listing on eBay, selling a 1-bedroom fixed week in their desired location for $1 (an amazing bargain), and the seller was even willing to pay the closing costs.

They did a thorough due diligence to investigate the deal, and make sure it was going to meet their needs. Their research showed that the resort was a good fit with their vacation style, and the timeshare was a good buy financially.

The purchase price was a bargain, and the annual maintenance fee of $635 fit well within their vacation budget. When they calculated the annual costs of ownership + the ability to get cheap extra vacations, they found that this purchase would save them money on vacations year after year.

---

* If you don't understand some of these terms, don't worry - we explain it all in detail in further sections of the book. For now, just focus on the difference in outcomes you can achieve. It's huge!

How can you win the game?

Be wary -- The problem with timeshares is that there are a lot of people who make a lot of money by convincing you to be on the losing side of the game. It's not paranoia to assume that the salesperson you're talking to is out to get you. There's no disputing the fact that many unsuspecting people are taken advantage of and ripped off. Be on your guard.

It's a shame -- The timeshare industry has more than its fair share of people willing to stretch the truth to grab your money, and scams are a dime a dozen. Timeshare salespeople are right up there with guys selling used cars as far as trustworthiness goes. The standard joke is "if the salesman's lips are moving, then he's lying." It's not quite that bad in reality (there are some honest salespeople), but it's too close to the mark for comfort. It's a shame that companies have allowed it to reach this point, but they have.

The benefits are there -- On the other hand, there are tremendous benefits for people in the know, who have learned how to avoid the scams, find the deals, and buy the bargains. You really can find deals that save you thousands (or tens of thousands) of dollars. You really can get budget vacations your family will enjoy for years to come. You really can get fabulous resort vacations around the world. The potential benefits are real.

The key to winning -- The key to winning is to play the game by your own rules, rather than playing it the way they want you to. Just as in Las Vegas, the odds are stacked in favor of the house. If you do what they want, they'll always win. You need to change the game, and play it your own way instead.

Your first step to winning -- Read this book. We're not selling timeshares, and don't make anything by convincing you to buy one. Our goal is to level the playing field, by giving you the inside secrets the resorts don't want you to know. Don't be a helpless pawn, forking over your money to a smooth talking salesperson. Learn the techniques in this book, and become an educated buyer who knows how to work the system. Before long, you will be Winning the Timeshare Game.

Insider tip: What if you already paid too much? -- Perhaps you already bought a timeshare from the developer at retail price, and realize you paid far too much. If this happened in the last few days or if you were a victim of fraud, you might be able to get out of the contract. Otherwise you're on the hook, and it's yours. So what to do?

First of all, don't kick yourself too much over it. Timeshare salespeople are highly skilled in manipulation and persuasion, and have convinced millions of people to do the same thing you did. It's not your fault that you fell for it.

Next, realize that there was a grain of truth in the sales pitch. There were reasons you found the offer so appealing that you were willing to spend a lot of money on it. Many owners paid full price for a timeshare, spending far more than necessary, yet still enjoy their timeshares.

Why not make the most of it? Through a combination of using your timeshare, exchanging it, and making use of add-on opportunities like extra vacations, you can get real benefit from it. If you need to recoup some of your costs, you can also look into renting it out. For tips on all of these strategies, see our companion book for timeshare owners, **Winning the Timeshare Game: Making the Most of Your Timeshare**.

2. Timeshare Fundamentals

What is a timeshare?

Imagine this. . . You're sitting on the beach at your resort on Maui, while the kids build sandcastles nearby. The snorkeling this morning was awesome, with a couple of enormous sea turtles putting in an appearance, much to everyone's delight. Now it's time to relax, and you're sipping a Mai Tai, complete with the little paper umbrella that's a sure sign you're on vacation. After dinner, you can all go back to your condo for a family movie night in the living room. Once the kids are tucked in and sleeping soundly in their bedroom, the two of you can sit on the lanai, listening to the waves below.

How great would it be to own a condo in Hawaii and vacation like this?

Of course, most of us can't afford to buy a condo on Maui as a second home, but what if you could split the cost of the condo with a bunch of friends? You could each put in part of the cost, and use the unit part of the time.

Thus the concept of timeshares was born. The basic idea of a timeshare is that you and a bunch of other people share the time and the cost of a vacation property.

You could do this on your own with a group of your friends, but that can lead to thorny disagreements and bad feelings. You'd have to find a property that suits everybody's family size, vacation preferences, and budget, and that's just the start. Who decides about furnishings and decor? Who's responsible for dealing with maintenance issues? Who gets to use it during prime times like summer vacation or Christmas holidays? What if one person wants out of the deal after a couple of years? Questions like these can easily damage a friendship.

Instead of doing it yourself, the timeshare industry makes these arrangements for you. You purchase your right to use a property for part of the time (typically one week a year), and other people buy the rights to use it the rest of the time. Usually the property is a fully furnished condo at a vacation resort, which comes with everything from sheets to dishes to a DVD player. For an annual maintenance fee, the company handles all cleaning, repairs, and upgrades to the property.

Unfortunately, while this solves some problems for you, there are plenty of other potential issues you need to watch out for. Read on, and we'll help you navigate the minefield.

Vacationing in a timeshare vs. a hotel

Timeshares go by different names. You may see these called vacation clubs, destination clubs, fractional ownership, or vacation ownership. Details vary, but the concept is still the same.

Most timeshares are located in popular vacation destinations, so you'll find a lot of them in Florida (23% of US timeshares), Hawaii and Las Vegas, but not so many in Detroit. Timeshares are a worldwide business now, so there are timeshares in Europe, Australia, South America, and just about anywhere that lots of people go for vacation.

Usually, the property is a fully furnished resort condominium, complete with kitchen. You can get different size units depending on your needs, from a studio unit that sleeps two people, to a multi-bedroom unit that handles a group of 8 or 10. At some locations, the units are just like hotel rooms, but the condo arrangement is more common.

Having your own apartment instead of just a hotel room is a great benefit. In a hotel room, you're often limited to watching TV sitting on the bed, while a timeshare gives you a living room so you can spread out and get comfortable.

The extra space is especially important when you have a family. A two bedroom timeshare gives you a bedroom for the kids that's attached but still private, a master bedroom for the parents, and a living room and dining area. It's roomy enough that you can all enjoy spending time there together.

 Insider tip: Kitchens are great for the budget -- Having your own kitchen is a nice convenience, even if only for snacks and drinks, but the savings really add up when you use it for meals. You can cook full meals for the family, since most timeshares have pots and pans, utensils, and everything you need (including a dishwasher). Even if you just stock the fridge with orange juice and milk for simple breakfasts on your own, you save both the time and cost of eating out each morning. Having your own kitchen can lead to significant savings on the cost of a vacation.

Resort amenities depend on the property, but can be extensive, and comparable to an upscale hotel. You may find multiple swimming pools and jacuzzis, a golf course, restaurants, outdoor grills you can use, children's playgrounds, a game room or arcade, or a library where you can borrow books or DVDs. Often there is a schedule of events, with activities designed for both kids and adults. Many units include a washer and dryer, so you can easily do laundry during your stay.

If you're traveling as a couple, the two of you may appreciate the extra living space and having a kitchen.

If your whole family is vacationing together, then both space and money become even more important. A timeshare can be a comfortable and cost-conscious way to enjoy a wonderful family holiday.

Types of timeshare ownership

Deeded vs. Right to Use

Deeded Unit -- This is the most straightforward arrangement. You actually own a specific unit in the resort, for a specific interval of time. For example, you could receive a deed saying you own unit #309 for week 37 each year. You own this forever, just like you would own other real estate, though the contract may just give you ownership of the apartment, not any portion of the land on which it's built. You pay real estate taxes on this property (often bundled into the annual maintenance fee), and you can pass it on to your heirs. Deeded ownership is sometimes called "fee simple".

Right to Use -- With this type of contract, you do not actually own any real estate. Instead, you own the right to use the property, for a given amount of time each year. This right continues for a given period of time, and expires at the end of the contract. For example, you could have the right to use a 2-bedroom unit for one week each year, for the next 25 years. At the end of that 25 year period, all rights would revert to the property owner. With right to use timeshares, you may still have to pay property taxes, which will normally be included in your maintenance fee.

Undivided Interest -- In this case, you own a tiny fraction of the resort, but it's a non-specific interest. Rather than owning unit #309 for week 37, you might own 0.08% of the undivided total resort, with no specific unit or time period. This is typically combined with a right to use contract. You could own 0.08% undivided interest, along with the right to use a 2-bedroom unit for one week per year, or points that give you an equivalent benefit.

Vacation Club -- A vacation club is normally a right to use arrangement, where you don't own a resort property at all, but rather buy a club membership that gives you the right to use several different resorts. The club is run by trustees who control the resort properties. There are a couple of variations:

Club with Deeded Trust -- The trustees for the vacation club hold the deeds to the property, and you own a portion of that trust. In this case, if the vacation club went bankrupt, the typical process would be for the club and its assets to be bought by another company, so your timeshare rights would continue, but under a new company.

Alert: Club with Non-deeded Trust -- In this situation, the trustees run the vacation club, but they do not hold deeds to the property. If the club goes bankrupt, it doesn't actually own the property, and neither do you. Timeshare owners in clubs like this have been left with nothing when the club went bankrupt. If you paid $1 for your timeshare, who cares? Your maintenance fees go away with that $1 investment. But if you paid $20,000, that's a huge loss!

Weeks vs. points

Weeks -- In a system based on weeks, you buy a unit (or the right to use a unit) for a week each year. A week is the most common time interval, but it can vary. Some timeshares give you 2 weeks a year, a month a year, or a week every other year. If you pay for a week, that's what you get - a one-week vacation at this resort. You can exchange your week to stay at a different resort (more about exchanges later), and the trading power of your unit will depend on the desirability of your resort, unit, and week.

Points -- Many resorts now use a vacation ownership system based on points instead of weeks. Rather than buying "1 week", you buy "50,000 points" (the number varies considerably). You use the points to book your vacation time at your home resort or a different affiliated resort, or exchange them through a network. Different resorts, seasons and units will cost different numbers of points to book.

Note: Either Weeks or Points can be Deeded or Right to Use. For example, you can buy into a vacation club that gives you a deed to a share in the undivided real property at a resort, together with a set of points that you use to book your holiday stays. In other plans, you don't actually own part of any specific property, you just have points that give you the right to book a vacation.

Fixed vs. floating

Fixed -- A fixed week gives you the right to use your unit for a specific time period each year. For instance, you might own week 31 each year (where week 1 is the first week in the year). This would put your week in early August, ideal if you want to have a family vacation there each summer when the kids are out of school. Typically this August week would cost more than a week in October (when demand is lower), and less than Christmas week (which is often the most expensive).

Floating -- Instead of owning a fixed week, you can select from weeks during a given season. For instance, you might own a Summer week (usable in June through August), or a Fall week (usable September through November). If you purchase a week for prime season, you'll pay more than a week for off season. Within your time slot, whoever books first gets the weeks they want, so if you want a particular holiday, you need to move quickly. Seasons and weeks are commonly color coded to indicate demand. See more in *Timeshare seasons*.

Rotating -- (Unusual) Your week rotates through the calendar, so that everyone has equal access to the best weeks. If you have week 16 in one year, you'd have week 17 the next year, then 18, etc. While this makes it "fair" for everyone, it's quite inflexible, and you could wait for years before your week rotates around into the summer.

Lottery -- (Unusual) Some properties have gone to a lottery system, where everyone submits their choices for the weeks they want, and then a drawing determines who actually gets their first choices. Competition can be steep for peak summer season and holidays, and you may find that years go by when you cannot get what you want.

Timeshare seasons

Most resorts have the year broken into different seasons, based on patterns of demand. High season is when the most people want to stay there, and it costs more this time of year. Low or Off season has the lowest demand, and is the cheapest. Mid or Shoulder season is in between.

Definitions vary by location -- The calendar for each resort determines which weeks fall into which seasons. February could be High season at a ski resort, and Low season at a beach resort. It all depends on the demand - when do the most people want to visit?

Color coding -- Timeshare seasons are often color coded to indicate demand. Different companies use different color codes, which can be confusing. The most common designation is Red = High season. Thus, you'll frequently see "Red week" to indicate a floating week in the prime season.

	RCI *	Interval Int'l *	Other
High season	Red	Red	Platinum
Mid (Shoulder)	White	Yellow	Gold
Low (Off)	Blue	Green	Silver

* RCI and Interval International are the two largest timeshare exchange companies.

Seasons with weeks -- When you buy a floating week, you usually buy into one of these seasons. If you want the cheapest deal, you can buy a week in Low season, which gives you the right to stay there one of the weeks defined as Low season. If you want to be able to stay there at the most popular time of the year, then you pay more to buy a week in High season.

Seasons with points -- If you buy points rather than weeks, then the seasons still apply, but operate differently. You own a fixed number of points, and can spend them when you want. It will cost you more points to stay during high season than it will during low season. You might be able to get a large unit in low season, but only a smaller unit in high season.

Insider tip: Year round red -- Some resorts consider every week of the year to be a red week. This is the case with many resorts in Hawaii, Las Vegas, and some other places. While it's true that people do like to visit Hawaii year round, it's not really true that demand is the same every week of the year. For instance, families with kids in school can only vacation during school holidays, which creates a significant shift in demand. Though all the weeks are labeled "Red", some weeks are "Redder" than others, and will be more difficult to book.

There may be exclusions -- Sometimes specific weeks (especially holiday weeks) are excluded from the normal season calendar. Due to the very high demand for those specific weeks, they may be handled as fixed weeks, even in a floating calendar. For example, high season might not include Christmas week. If you own high season, you could go the week before or after Christmas, but not that specific week.

Insider tip: Escalating seasons -- Low season seems to be shrinking, as some companies escalate the seasons. You'll find that some points charts have 4 seasons specified, Low / Mid / High / Peak, with no dates falling into Low. In effect, you end up with the same three seasons, but now they're called Mid / High / Peak. It doesn't make much sense to have "Mid" at the bottom of the list, taking the dates that obviously are really low season. Perhaps it's their way to make those low season dates sound more appealing, or perhaps they can charge more if they don't call them "Low".

Timeshare exchange networks

When you buy a timeshare, you're usually buying vacations at a specific resort, but that doesn't mean it's the only place you can stay. One of the most attractive features of timeshares is the ability to trade to stay at a different property. With over 5,000 timeshare resorts around the world, you could easily stay in a different place each year.

Developer networks -- Most timeshares are part of a group of associated resorts run by the same developer, and you can exchange your unit or points for a stay at one of those locations. For instance, if you buy into the Marriott Vacation Club®, you can use your points to stay at Marriott vacation resorts.

Major exchange networks -- There are also extended timeshare networks that give you a bigger variety of resorts available for exchange. You pay an annual membership fee to join the network (as well as a fee to make an exchange), but you get access to thousands of destinations.

The major timeshare exchange networks are

RCI -- This is the largest timeshare network, with over 4,000 timeshare resorts in almost 100 countries available for you to choose. Current membership fees (subject to change) are $89 per year for weeks members, and $124 per year for points members. There are also assorted fees for exchanges and transactions - these vary, but a typical fee to exchange a week is $199.

Interval International -- This is the second largest timeshare network, with about 2,700 different destinations in 75 countries. Current membership fees (subject to change) are $84 per year, with a $139 fee to exchange a timeshare week within the US (more internationally).

Affiliated exchange networks -- Which of the major exchange networks you can use depends on which of them is affiliated with your resort. If you buy a timeshare in a resort that's affiliated with RCI, then you can join RCI to exchange for their properties. Likewise, if your resort is affiliated with Interval International, then you can join II and exchange through them. Most of the time you'll find that your home resort belongs to one of these major networks but not the other, though some resorts have affiliations with both.

Independent exchange networks -- There are also some smaller independent exchange networks. These are not affiliated with specific resorts, so they get people exchanging properties through them from a wide variety of companies. These smaller exchange companies don't have the reach or popularity of RCI or Interval International, but may have lower fees. See the section *Organizations and Resources* for a list of companies.

3. How THEY Want You to Buy a Timeshare

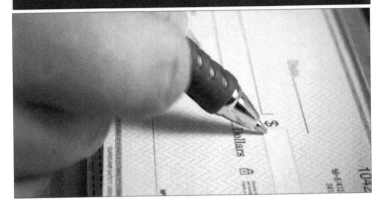

What to expect at a timeshare presentation

A timeshare sales presentation may be called a Resort Tour, or if you already own one timeshare, you may be invited to an Owner's Meeting. Regardless of what they call it, when you're meeting with representatives of the timeshare organization, their purpose is to sell you something and get your money.

Usually there is a gift or incentive involved. You may get anything from two nights free stay, to a free car rental or discount luau tickets. The catch is that you need to attend the Resort Tour (or whatever they call it) in order to get your freebie.

Don't walk into one of these sessions blind, or you could lose a lot of money. You are going to get the hard sell, and this could take a lot longer than you anticipate. It's not uncommon for a 60-minute tour to turn into a 5-hour marathon with multiple salespeople taking turns working on you. You need to keep your guard up and know how to say No, to make it out of this with your finances intact.

Insider tip: Do not buy now -- Don't buy anything at one of these sales presentations. There is a better way that will cost you a lot less, and we'll explain it all to you in this book. In the meantime, if you get stuck in one of these timeshare presentations, listen, but don't buy.

How a typical presentation works

Cheery start -- Usually there will be multiple people attending at the same time, and you will have a cheerful, friendly tour guide who greets you. There could be refreshments served, helping to get everyone in a good mood. You'll probably see a film about exotic destinations and luxurious resorts around the world (places you could visit if only you buy one of these timeshares). There are sure to be lots of smiling, laughing people in the video. Just think, you could be one of them.

Property tour -- Next, they'll take you on a tour of the property, and your guide will point out all of the special features and amenities that make this such a great place. You'll get to see one or more of the units, often selected to fit the needs of your family. The tour guide will often talk about what's great about the area too - fun activities, unique restaurants, etc. They want to be helpful and friendly, and bond with you.

The world is your oyster -- After the facility tour, you will end up back in a meeting room. Now you hear about all the other places you could go if you join their vacation club, and the thousands of resorts around the world where you can exchange your timeshare. They may pull out a book with pictures of fabulous exotic resorts, and ask you to start choosing which of them you'd like to visit.

Once you're all warmed up with thoughts of this wonderful resort, and dreams of the other places you could vacation, it's time for the selling to begin.

Down to business -- One person will let you know the full retail price of the unit they feel will best suit you and your family. In the US, this person usually has to be a Licensed Real Estate Agent, but rules vary in different places. If you're not jumping up and down to buy at the full retail price, then they will send in the big guns to sell you. In industry lingo, this is the T.O. or the Turn Over.

The hard sell -- One or more sales people will now try various approaches to get you to buy a timeshare, and buy it today. There will be discounts offered, arguments made, and lots and lots of selling. You could end up talking to one person for hours, or they may call over someone else if they're not making headway.

It goes on, and on, and on... -- This process goes on for hour after hour. Being in a timeshare sales meeting for 7 hours is not unheard of. This is exhausting, and unless you know what to expect and how to continue saying No, you may leave having spent way too much money on a full priced timeshare.

Tactics they may use on you

Would you agree that ____? -- This is designed to get you saying "Yes" to something. Salespeople know that once you say Yes to one thing, it's easier to get you to say Yes to something else, too. As an example, they might ask "Would you agree that a fabulous vacation is fun for your family?" How could you disagree with that? Now you're saying Yes, off to a good start.

Which is better, X or Y? -- This is so you'll acknowledge the benefits they're selling. For instance "Which is better - our exchange networks where you have 5,000 choices of resorts you can visit, or company Y, that offers far fewer options?" The answer is obvious, and it gets you to affirm that you think their product is superior.

Scam alert: This offer is only good today -- They want you to buy right now, while they have you in their clutches, before you can walk away and think about it clearly with no pressure. Timeshare salespeople will usually offer you a "special price that's only good today", to try to rush the issue. Don't believe it. They say the same thing every single day.

You take vacations anyway -- An important part of the sales pitch is that you spend money on vacations anyway, so you might as well spend that money on a timeshare. They'll try to get numbers from you that they can use in their arguments. Do you normally spend $3,000 per year on vacation? This will come back at you in calculations designed to persuade you that a $30,000 timeshare is a good idea. Don't give them financial information to work with.

Scam alert: You get prepaid vacations -- A common line is that your purchase price buys you prepaid vacations for years. That's not true. You do pay a lump sum up front, but all the purchase price gets you is the right to vacation at that resort - it doesn't cover the costs of the vacation. Your actual yearly vacation cost will include the Annual maintenance fees + Membership fees, taxes and usage fees + Transportation costs + Food and beverages + Activities and extras. None of these things are prepaid. Find more about this in the section *Calculating the true cost of a timeshare.*

Scam alert: This is an investment -- Timeshares are not like investing in other real estate. You cannot expect them to go up in value over time - it's quite the opposite. If it's a Right to Use property, then you don't actually own any property, and the contract may have an expiration date. Even if it's a Deeded unit, the value goes down 99.9% of the time. In this book, we'll teach you how to buy a resale timeshare for a bargain price, after some other unfortunate person lost a bundle of money on it.

Using your information -- Timeshare salespeople are highly skilled at using every piece of information you provide, and fitting it into tailored sales tactics. Did you mention that you'll be retiring in 10 years? That you just bought a new car? That you love scuba diving? That your brother-in-law owns a timeshare in Orlando? Whatever you tell them, expect that information to be brought back into the conversation in a way that's designed to get you to buy.

Scam alert: You can go anywhere, anytime -- This one overstates your real options and doesn't give you the whole story. Yes, you can exchange your timeshare for thousands of other resorts. However, you may easily find that your unit or points don't give you the trading power you need for the resort or time period you want. You may also find that what you want simply isn't available for exchange during peak seasons.

Other people are buying -- There are usually other potential buyers going through the same process you are, each meeting with a different salesperson. When one of them decides to buy, there may be a celebration, with people clapping or champagne corks popping. It's intended to make you think other people are getting in on a terrific deal, so that you'll want to do the same. Sometimes this is even faked - there's no real buyer, they're just pretending.

Let me ask my manager -- This is the old trick from car dealers. The salesperson says this is the best price they can get you, but has to ask their manager if there's anything better they can do. It's not real. They already know what deals they can offer.

Scam alert: Overpricing -- Whatever they tell you, you are guaranteed to be paying too much if you buy a timeshare from the developer for retail price. If they start out with a price of $60,000, and knock it down to $40,000 "just for you in a never-before-done special offer", don't fall for it. Chances are you could find the same thing on resale for a fraction of that price. You might find it on eBay for $4,000 or even $400.

Wearing you down -- Most people go to a timeshare presentation expecting it to be about an hour, but they often take much longer. In some cases, people have been there for 4 hours, and been told that it would be another 2 hours - unless they signed on the dotted line, in which case they could leave immediately.

Insider tip: You can walk out anytime -- You have the right to stand up and walk away any time you choose. You may not get the free gifts unless you stay for a designated length of time, but sometimes it's better to just get out. If you're feeling bullied, pressured, or backed into a corner, remember that you can walk away whenever you choose. They cannot legally hold you there against your will.

Saying No, No, No to the hard sell

No is the best answer. **Just say "No, I don't want it."**

Insider tip: Objections don't work -- You don't have to give reasons or excuses to justify why you don't want to purchase. In fact it's better if you don't. Timeshare salespeople are trained to discover your objections and then counter them, in order to get you to sign that sales contract. They have books and websites devoted to techniques for *overcoming every objection* you may raise, and many of these salespeople are highly skilled.

* If you say **"It's too expensive"**, they will counter with a cheaper unit or smaller number of points, discuss that you're spending money on vacations anyway, or offer you financing options.

* If you say **"I'm not sure I want to come back here every year"**, they will counter with exchange options, noting that you can go all over the world.

* If you say **"But what if I lose my job?"**, they can counter that prices are depressed now, while the economy is turning the corner, so there's no better time to buy.

* If you say **"I need the money for my daughter's college tuition"**, they will say it's wonderful that you're a conscientious parent, but remember that vacations are important, and this valuable timeshare will be good for your family.

* If you say **"But I already own a timeshare I'm happy with"**, they will counter with all the reasons this new option would be better than what you already own.

Get the picture?

The one word they can't counter? NO. Just be prepared to use it many times!

Skip the presentation or use it for research

By now, you have a good feel for the high pressure sales techniques that you will encounter at a timeshare presentation. They put on the pressure, and try angle after angle to convince you that you really need to buy this timeshare right now.

There are two approaches you can take:

- ☐ **Skip the presentation** -- Just give up the thought of that free car rental or discount luau they're offering, and save yourself the headache of sitting through this ordeal. If you're one of the billions of people who detest high pressure sales, or you're easily swayed by persuasive salespeople, then skipping the presentation is probably the best idea. There are better ways to buy a timeshare.

- ☐ **Attend, but just for research purposes** -- If you're certain that you can withstand the pressure they'll apply and stick with your resolve to NOT BUY ANYTHING, then you can go ahead and attend the presentation, knowing full well that you have no intention of buying anything.

If you are attending for research, then ask many questions. Make sure you understand exactly what they're selling, where and when this would let you vacation, how you reserve time slots at their resort, what all the costs are (both initial and on-going), and how exchanges work (including additional fees).

Read through the section *Considerations before you buy a timeshare*, and make a list of questions before you get to the presentation. Ask all your questions, and be prepared to say No, No, No.

Insider tip: Things to know before you go -- Here are a couple of VERY useful points to research before you walk into any timeshare presentation. Their pressure-packed sales techniques won't have nearly the power if you're pre-armed with these tidbits.

1) Resale prices. Do a quick search on eBay and Redweek.com, and find out what resale values are for the resort you're visiting, and other similar properties nearby. It's great to walk into a presentation knowing you could get the same thing for a fraction of the price the salesman is quoting.

2) Rescission laws. Most states in the US, and some other countries, have a mandatory Rescission Period (the official term for a "cooling off period"). This lets you cancel your contract within a certain number of days of the sale. Before you sign any contract, it's smart to know whether or not you could get out of it. See the next section for more on rescission.

If you choose to skip the presentation to save your sanity, there are other ways to research. It may take longer than attending the presentation and asking questions, but you can relax rather than having your defenses up for an afternoon of selling. You'll also get more unbiased information when you research on your own rather than relying on what a salesperson tells you.

Fall for the hard sell? You may have an out

Most places in the United States have a mandatory "cooling off" period for timeshare sales, called a **Rescission Period**. This is for your protection when dealing with high-powered sales people, who may talk you into a deal that's not good for you.

The way it works is that you have a certain number of days after you make your purchase to change your mind. If you realize the next day that this purchase is just too expensive or not right for you, then you can cancel the contract and get your deposit back.

Normally the rescission period will be stated directly on the contract. The salesperson may not mention it, because of course they don't want you to rescind the contract. You need to know your own rights on this one.

In the US, the rescission period varies by state, from 0 (no rescission) to 15 days. See the section *Timeshare rescission periods by US state* for details. If you are considering a property outside the US, you need to research what the laws are there. In some countries, you will have fewer consumer protections and no guaranteed rescission period.

What are your rights if the salesman lied?

If you were coerced or lied to during your sales presentation, then you may be able to cancel your contract due to fraud. Once again, your protections will depend on what jurisdiction you are in, but in the US, you are generally protected from deceptive business practices. The signed contract is the binding document, however, and it may be difficult to prove what was said but never written down.

First of all, see if you are within the Rescission Period. If you are, then immediately take steps to rescind your contract. This is the easiest way to get out of it. You need to follow specific steps to notify the company in writing that you're rescinding the deal, and you'll get out of the contract, with your money refunded. **Time is of the essence, so move fast**.

If you're past the rescission period (or if there isn't one), then you will need to try to get out of the contract due to fraud and misrepresentation. Most states in the US have laws preventing deceptive trade practices, and this is what you'll be relying on.

Insider tip: Get it down on paper -- As soon as possible, make a list of lies and distortions from your sales presentation. Be as detailed as you can in recording who said what during the conversation. Your memory of the details is apt to fade over time, so it's best to record what happened while it's fresh in your mind.

At this point, you will need to begin action against the timeshare company to get out of the deal. If you have some proof of the lies you were told (anything recorded or in writing), then your chances of winning this are much better. If it's just your word vs. their word, then you may not be so lucky.

For more details on how to cancel either via Rescission or for Fraud, see our companion book for people who want to sell or cancel their timeshares, **Winning the Timeshare Game - Getting Out**.

4. How YOU Want to Buy a Timeshare

Standard path (theirs) vs. Alternate path (yours)

After reading about timeshare presentations and the often sleazy practices there, you may feel like all timeshares are a rip-off. That's definitely not the case. Many people enjoy timeshare vacations year after year, and are very happy with their purchases. The key is how you play the game.

Standard path -- If you pay a retail price of $25,000 for a timeshare, plus the associated annual fees, then it's hard to figure out the math that makes that a good purchase. If you have to sell it for $500 after a few years, then you've lost a lot of money. You'll probably be out telling your friends what a scam timeshares are, and feel justifiably bitter about the whole experience.

Alternate path -- On the other hand, if you are the person who picks that same timeshare up for $500, the equation is totally different. Your investment is a lot less, and the transaction makes far more sense financially. This can easily be an economical way for you and your family to vacation for years. You'll probably be bragging to friends about the great deal you got, and feel like a timeshare winner.

The key is to play the game on your own terms. Don't fall for buying timeshares at retail prices from the developer, no matter what lines they use on you. You can take the alternate path, and buy the same thing for a fraction of the price.

If you're worried about buying "new vs. used", then relax. It's not like a used car, where the previous owner could have trashed it. Your timeshare unit is maintained by the resort just like all the others, and has other people staying there the rest of the year. It's like airline pricing, where the person in the seat next to you could have paid far more (or less) than you did. In this case, the person staying in this same unit the week after you could have paid quite a different price.

Key question: Which way will you go? -- Do you follow the standard path they want you to, or take your own approach? Your financial outcome will be much different one way than the other!

Success Story - A timeshare for $1

In 2012, I bought a 2-bedroom, one week, deeded timeshare at the Sedona Summit for $1, from timeshareaz.com.

Yes, it was just $1, plus closing costs and transfer fees of $400. This was an amazing deal, since the resort was currently selling points for a two bedroom unit for over $25,000.

As a resale week, my timeshare does not include membership in the Diamond Resorts Club, which means I can't make internal exchanges within Diamond International. The hidden benefit here is that it also means I don't have to pay the club membership fee of $299/year.

What I can do is exchange this timeshare with either RCI or Interval International, and I know from experience that these units trade very well.

The 2-bedroom is a lock-off, so I can split it and deposit the two smaller units into RCI, each with enough trading power to get me a week's stay at many other resorts. This lets me trade my 1 week at Sedona for 2 separate weeks at other resorts. All for $1, instead of $25,000!

Key takeaways:

1) You can save a lot of money when you don't pay retail!

2) When you buy a resale timeshare, there may be some limitations on it. The thousands of dollars you save, however, are worth a lot more than the features you may be missing.

Where to find timeshare bargains

There are a number of avenues you can explore when looking for bargain timeshares. Check out this list, and you'll start to see what's available.

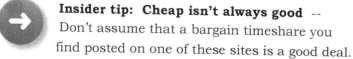

Insider tip: Cheap isn't always good -- Don't assume that a bargain timeshare you find posted on one of these sites is a good deal. Even a timeshare offered for $1 may have problems that mean you're better off not buying it. You need to do your own research and evaluate each opportunity. Other sections in this book cover all the details on how to do that.

Developer or Resort Association -- Usually these folks are pushing overpriced retail units, but in some cases, they may handle resales too. They will still take a hefty commission, but it's less than buying at full retail. If you're interested in a particular resort, ask if they have an office that handles resales. If so, then see what resales they're offering. If you find something you like here, then still check for comparison prices on other sites (see below). A resale office at a resort can also be useful in the future when you're ready to sell.

Redweek.com -- This is a popular website for people who want to buy, sell, or rent timeshares around the world. Prices range from $0 to over $20,000. If you find something you like, you buy it directly from the owner. They have about 1.5 million users, so it's a sizable community. It's free to browse listings and see what's available. If you want to read resort reviews or contact an owner about a sale, it costs $15 per year for a membership. *redweek.com*

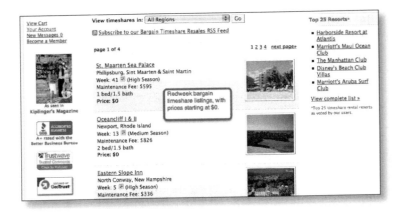

eBay -- You can find pretty much anything on eBay, including timeshares. Just go to eBay and search for "timeshares for sale", and you'll see quite a list of them. You won't find resort reviews here, but you can research those elsewhere. What you will find is some great bargains, with some timeshares listed at just $0.01. The previous owners are probably losing a bundle on these, but their loss could be your gain. *ebay.com*

Timeshare Users' Group (TUG) -- This site has an active forum for timeshare owners to discuss everything about timeshares. It also has resort reviews, and a classified ad system, where owners can post their own timeshares for sale or rent. Sometimes you'll even find people giving their units away for free. The membership is $15 per year, and well worth it for the information you can find here. *tug2.net*

Timeshare Adventures -- This company says they use an in-house timeshare attorney to manage the sales process, dealing with both the seller and the resort. There are plenty of timeshares for sale here, in a wide range of prices. Some are good deals, while others seem almost as expensive as buying retail. *timeshareadventures.com*

Timesharing Today -- This magazine for timeshare owners includes classified ads for people reselling their timeshares. You can see the ads on the website, even if you're not a magazine subscriber. There isn't much information conveyed in each listing, but it's another place to check when comparison shopping. *tstoday.com*

Timeshare Resales Worldwide -- This web-based business uses licensed real estate brokers to handle resales of timeshares. They have thousands of listings for properties in the US and other countries. There's limited information available online, but you can fill out a form for more information, or submit a bid online. *alltimeshare.com*

Craigslist -- People do post ads for timeshares for sale on Craigslist, so you might be able to find a bargain here. The site is not as user friendly as Redweek (with resort reviews) or eBay (with seller feedback), so you'll have to make extra sure on your due diligence. That said, there are bargains to be had here. *craigslist.org*

Google -- If there's a specific resort you're interested in, then google the resort name, and see what turns up. There are quite a few resellers like Smart Choice Timeshare Resales (*timeshareaz.com*), who specialize in specific regions or timeshare companies. If you google the resort you want, you may find various people selling it.

How the buying process works

Buying from the resort -- If you're buying a timeshare from a developer resale office or a licensed real estate broker who is experienced with timeshares, then they will be used to managing this process, and will have one or more title companies who they regularly deal with.

Buying from the owner -- If you're purchasing directly from an owner via Redweek, eBay or elsewhere, then you and the seller will need to organize the transfer process. The safest and simplest way to manage this is to go through a title company that has experience with timeshares.

Using a title company -- A title company can handle escrow for the entire deal, so that you put your money into escrow with the title company, the sales process takes place (over a number of weeks), and once the transfer is successfully completed, the funds are released to the seller. This provides a measure of safety to both buyer and seller.

How the process works -- Using a title company and escrow is the safest method of arranging the deal, with escrow services protecting the interests of both buyer and seller. If you go this route, here's how it works.

1) **Agree on price and terms** -- Make sure you and the seller are in agreement about the important things before you close the deal. This includes selling price, costs due at closing (and who's paying those closing costs), and using a title company and escrow service.

2) **Select a title company** -- Buyer and seller agree on a title company to use for the process. Most title companies will also provide escrow services.

3) **Fund escrow** -- Buyer puts funds into escrow with the title company. For large purchase prices, this may be split into a down payment now and final payment later.

4) **Prepare documents** -- The title company prepares the necessary deeds and documents, and gets signatures from both parties as needed.

5) **Title search and insurance** -- If you are purchasing title insurance, then the company will do a title search and issue insurance.

6) **Transfer with the resort** -- Title company records the transfer with the timeshare resort or points program. This will require paying a resort transfer fee.

7) **Record with the government** -- If the timeshare is a deeded property, then the title company also files the change of ownership with the appropriate government agency (typically a County Recorder in the US). There will also be a recording fee here.

8) **Finish the deal** -- Once all transfers are complete and recorded, the title company releases the money to the seller, and gives ownership documents to the buyer. If a deed was filed with the county, then you may also receive a copy of the recorded deed directly from the county.

Do-It-Yourself approach -- A seller may want you to pay them directly, and then give you a grant deed or quitclaim deed. If you go this route without using a title company, it means that you need to ensure everything is recorded correctly with the appropriate people. It also leaves you open to potential problems that can occur during the transfer. Using a title company does involve paying their fee, but it makes the process safer and easier.

What are the costs? This will vary depending on your transaction, the location, and the parties involved. Generally, the up front purchase costs will include the sale price, closing costs, a resort transfer fee, and various additional fees. There are also on-going maintenance fees and taxes. All of these costs are covered in depth in the section *Fees, fees, fees...*

Insider tip: Will the seller cover closing costs? -- Sometimes a motivated seller will be willing to cover the closing costs, or split the expense with the buyer. This can be part of your negotiations before you finalize the sale.

Should you get title insurance? This is a question for you to decide, based on how much you have at risk in the purchase. If you're buying a timeshare for one dollar, it doesn't make much sense to pay $200-300 more for title insurance. On the other hand, if you're shelling out thousands, this does ensure your title is free and clear, and protects you from title issues that could cause you to lose your investment.

Selecting a title company -- It's safest if you do a little research, and select a title company yourself. Make sure they are licensed, bonded, and experienced with timeshares. One approach is to find out what title company the resort normally uses, and go with them. The advantage is that they will be used to the resort's procedure and the paperwork involved.

Insider tip: This could take awhile -- This process could take anywhere from a week to a few months to complete the deal. Some companies move astonishingly slowly in completing the transfer, and if there's any little discrepancy along the way, it can hold things up for weeks. Don't assume you'll be able to use your new timeshare right away.

Insider tip: Get the seller to make you a reservation -- Since it could take weeks or months for your deal to close, your vacation opportunities by that time will be limited, as other people snap up the best time slots. One option is to see if the seller can reserve a week for you while they still control the timeshare, then you get the use of that week when the deal is done.

For example, say you're buying a timeshare in Jan, and the seller has already paid the annual maintenance fees, so that you're getting a free year of use. You'd like to get a summer vacation, but those weeks may be fully booked by Feb or Mar, when your deal closes. See if the seller can reserve a summer week for you, since they can get their request in sooner.

5. Considerations When Buying a Timeshare

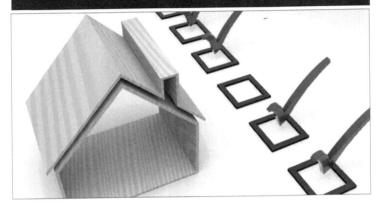

Renting a timeshare vs. buying

Timeshare resorts often rent out units when they're not booked by owners, so you may be able to stay at a resort without the on-going commitment of purchasing a unit. If you could vacation at the same resort either renting or buying, which would be better?

Which is cheaper, renting or buying? Use the section *Calculating the true cost of a timeshare* to figure out how much it would cost you to vacation in this timeshare as an owner. Then check out rental rates for this resort, either from the resort website itself, or on a site like Expedia. Is it cheaper to own or to rent?

It's important to compare apples to apples here. Are you paying for a high-demand week during the peak summer season, or for an off-season week that goes for a lower price? Whatever season you're targeting, make sure you're looking at the same thing for both renting and owning.

Availability (or lack of) -- If you want to vacation at a popular resort at a desirable time of year, is it available for rentals? Often the best times are booked up by owners. Could you get the time you want by buying a timeshare? Even if you own at a resort but have a floating week or points, it may be difficult to get prime time slots. If you're looking for something like

Christmas week, the only way to make absolutely sure you get it is to buy a fixed week.

Key question: How much advanced planning can you do? -- For a fixed week timeshare, your vacation will always fall at the same time of year. If you purchase a floating week timeshare or points, then the further in advance you make your plans, the better your chances of getting what you want. If your lifestyle makes planning vacations many months in advance difficult, then you may not get maximum value from owning a timeshare. If that's your situation, you may prefer the flexibility of renting.

What exactly are you buying?

This seems like a simple question, but the timeshare industry has developed so many convoluted variations that it's not as easy as it seems.

Type of purchase -- A fundamental question is whether you're buying a specific type of unit for a specific interval of time (buying weeks), or buying points that you can exchange to stay in a unit (buying points). Which is better is a matter of debate, and is explored more in the section below, *Which is better - weeks or points?*

Type of unit -- Either way, you need to know what rights you'll have to stay at this resort. Are you buying a studio, a 1-bedroom, or a 2-bedroom unit? If you're buying points, what kind of unit will those points get you? How many people can stay there? Have you seen the units themselves, or at least the floor plans, so you know what they're like?

Fixed unit or variable -- Are you buying a specific unit, a certain category of units, or will you get whatever unit is available when you visit? Do you always get unit #1017, always get a unit with an ocean view, or will you sometimes get one with a view of the parking lot?

Time period -- Do you get use of the unit one week per year (most common), one week every other year, or some other period? Can you use it any time of year, or are you buying into a specific week or season?

Ownership type -- Are you buying a deeded unit, or is it a right to use contract? With a deeded unit, you actually own a piece of the resort (though perhaps not the land it's built on). With right to use contracts, do you have a right to use specifically at this resort, or is it a membership in a vacation club that covers multiple resorts?

Expiration date -- Are you buying this forever (typical with a deeded unit), or does the contract have an expiration date (often the case with right to use contracts)? If there is an expiration date, how close is it?

Which is better - weeks or points?

How weeks work -- You purchase either a fixed or floating week at a resort, which you can use each year (in the most common scenario), in a certain type of unit. For instance, you might own a 2-bedroom unit for a week in high season. If you want to stay at a different place, then you exchange your week for a week at another resort. What you can exchange for depends on what you own. The better the week you own (resort desirability, season, and unit), the better you can expect to get as an exchange.

Industry changes -- In the early days of timeshares, people bought specific fixed weeks to use their units. What this meant for developers was that it was easy to sell the weeks for high season, and those went for premium prices. The weeks for low season were more difficult to sell. Lots of people want to visit Arizona as a winter escape, but who wants to go to Scottsdale when it's 118 degrees outside?

This system evolved to selling floating weeks, so they could sell people the ability to use the resort all year round, leaving it up to different time allocation schemes to determine who gets what weeks. This flexible ownership plan was taken to the next level by selling points, rather than a single week in a specific type of unit.

How points work -- A points membership gives you a list of related resorts where you can use your points. Each stay you want to reserve costs a different amount of points, based on a points chart that considers resort popularity, time of year, type of unit, and length of stay. If you want to extend your vacation, or visit a more expensive resort than your points cover, you can buy (or sometimes borrow or rent) additional points to make up the difference. You may also be able to use your points for airline tickets, car rentals, cruises or hotels (though it's not usually a good deal to do this).

Points are less like owning a piece of a resort, and more like having cash in your bank account that you can use where you like.

Both Weeks and Points have their pros and cons, and some people will swear by each system. The table below gives a brief rundown.

	Weeks	Points
Pros	1) Clarity. You know exactly what you own, especially with a fixed unit and/or fixed week. 2) Guaranteed availability, if you own a fixed week. 3) Permanence. They can't change the rules in the future to say you only own 6 nights instead of 7.	1) Variety. You've got a list of resorts where you can use your points, not just one resort. 2) Flexibility. You aren't tied to a certain type of unit, or to stays of 7 nights. Each vacation can be different. You can also use points for cruises, rental cars, etc.
Cons	1) You're usually tied to full week stays, which might not always be convenient. 2) Tied to a location. If you want to stay somewhere else, you need to go through an exchange and pay exchange fees.	1) It's not as clear what you own - what does 10,000 points mean? It takes a little work to understand it. 2) Value can change. 10,000 points could equate to a summer week in a 1BR, but in the future it might change to 12,000.

	Weeks	Points
What if you can't use it one year?	If you can't use your week one year, you can rent it out to someone else, or deposit (bank) it with an exchange company.	Different companies have different rules about depositing (banking), expiring, extending, or renting your points.

Scam alert: "Upgrading" gives you less -- Current weeks owners at a location that also does points, may be asked to an Owner's Meeting when they stay at their own resort.. This is really another timeshare sales presentation, where they want to sell you an "upgrade" to convert your week into points. Of course this means paying more money. Watch out, because you may end up with less. Some people have been known to trade in their unit for 10,000 points and pay additional cash for this "upgrade", only to find that it takes 15,000 points to get a week in the same unit that they just traded in.

When can you use it?

Weeks - Fixed or Float? -- If you always like to vacation at a specific time, perhaps due to school schedules, or you want a premium week like Christmas, then buying a fixed week is the best way to ensure that you always get it. If you're happy to move your vacation schedule around, a floating system has more flexibility.

Insider tip: Systems to avoid -- Avoid places selling timeshare weeks with Rotating or Lottery systems. You could wait a long time to get the schedule you want. These aren't very common and there's a good reason for that.

Red weeks, Blue weeks, etc. -- These terms were created to reflect the fact that some weeks of the year are in higher demand than others. "Red week" commonly refers to a high-demand week, and you pay more for high-season weeks than for low-season weeks. See the section *Timeshare seasons* for more on this.

Different places have different rules if you bought a high-demand "red week". You might be able to use this any time of year, or you might only be able to use it during specified "red weeks". If you're buying a timeshare, make sure you know the terminology for your resort, and when you'll be able to use it.

When can you not use it? -- Sometimes there are exclusions like holiday weeks. Even if you bought a red week on a floating plan, it may not cover Christmas, which is sometimes handled as a fixed week, even if the rest of the year is floating.

How far in advance can you reserve? -- Unless you have a fixed week, the most popular times tend to fill up fast, on a first come first served, basis. If you are able to plan far in advance, this can be good for you. As soon as things open up for reservations, book it, and you can probably get what you want.

Key question: Are you a last-minute person? -- If your lifestyle isn't conducive to much advance planning, this makes it more difficult for you to book the best times of year in a timeshare, whether you own a floating week or points system. There may be last minute openings, but usually the best slots fill up early. If you really want to stay at that ski resort when there's snow on the ground, you probably need to book early. If you're happy to stay there May or October, there's not as much lead time required.

How does it work with points? When you buy points, the key to knowing where you can stay and when all lies in the "Points chart". Every resort in a points system has a chart that shows you how many points it costs to book various size units, during different times of the year.

For instance, you might find that your points are enough to book you a week in a 1BR unit at the beach resort you want in peak season, or a 2BR unit at the same resort in off season. Each place has a different points chart, so the same points might only get you 3 days instead of a week at another resort.

Even though you're buying points, in some systems, you still buy into a "home week", which is a specific type of unit, in a specific season, at a specific resort. You can use your points however you want, but you get first crack at booking your home week, before everyone else gets a chance. If you want to book a high-demand period, this can be a big help to getting the time slot you want.

Insider tip: Finding the points chart -- Some timeshare companies don't want to make their points charts visible to the public until after you purchase a timeshare. Even though seeing what you can get with your points is a primary consideration in deciding to buy, they like to keep that information secret. You can get around this by doing a Google search for the points chart, or looking through the forum on TUG (the Timeshare Users' Group). Usually you can find the information you need somewhere online.

Where can you exchange?

It's good to have your home resort somewhere that you love to visit, because that is the most economical way to use your timeshare. Even if you adore your home resort, though, there will be years when you'd like to do something different. This is where exchanges come in.

You can exchange your week (or points) to stay at a different resort. Where you can exchange will depend on where you bought your timeshare. Different resorts are affiliated with different networks.

Developer network or Vacation club -- If you buy a resort that's a member of a group, then you usually have special rights to stay at resorts that are part of that group. For instance, if you're part of Hilton Grand Vacations, then you have special rights to stay at the properties that are part of that club. If you bought into the Starwood Vacation Network, then you can stay at the resorts that are part of that network.

Insider tip: Resales may come with limitations -- Sometimes if you buy a resale timeshare, the company will put limitations on your ownership and exchange options. For example, if you buy a Marriott resale unit from a third party, then you can't use Marriott Rewards Points exchanges - you can only do that if you buy direct from the company. It's good to know the rules, but generally this doesn't have much impact compared to the thousands (or tens of thousands) of dollars you can save by buying a third party resale. After all, there are other ways you can exchange your timeshare.

Exchange network -- Virtually every timeshare resort will also be affiliated with a large exchange network that gives you access to thousands of resort properties around the world. The two largest are RCI and Interval International.

RCI -- (Resort Condominiums International) This is the largest timeshare exchange network in the world, with over 4,000 properties in about 100 countries. This exchange network is known for having the most options, and its properties vary from basic to upscale. *rci.com*

Interval International -- This is the second largest timeshare network, with about 2,700 different destinations in 75 countries. It's known for having higher quality resorts than RCI on average, but RCI does have some premium resorts as well. *intervalworld.com*

Usually you'll find that your resort is part of either RCI or Interval International. You can only join and exchange through the company affiliated with your resort.

Insider tip: Dual exchange networks -- Some resorts are part of both RCI and II. Such a dual-exchange property gives you the most trading options, though you would have to pay two membership fees to use both networks. You can only deposit your week/points into one or the other, but paying for both for a year lets you check them both out and learn what each system can offer you.

Independent exchange networks -- RCI and II are the largest exchange companies, but there are others, too. See *Timeshare exchange companies* in the *Additional Resources* section near the end of this book.

How much trading power will you get?

Trading power or exchange value is a measure of how much your timeshare is worth, compared to other resorts that you'd like to trade for. The more valuable and in demand your unit is, the easier it is to trade it for other locations.

Using Points, it's fairly simple. If you have 20,000 points, you can look at a points chart to see what units that would get you in different seasons at different resorts. More expensive destinations, more luxurious resorts, larger units, peak time periods, and longer stays will require more points.

Using Weeks, your trading power will depend on the relative value of your home resort, as well as the size of your unit, the desirability of your week, and how far in advance you deposit it. If you have a fixed week, then you know whether you have a high demand week or not. If you have a float week, the exchange value of your week can vary.

In general, expect to trade for something on a par with what you own. If you have a high-demand week at an upscale resort in a popular destination, then you'll have a wide range of trade opportunities. Don't expect to trade an off-season studio at a basic resort for a 2BR luxury unit on the beach in Hawaii.

For more on how to make the best use of your trading power and exchanges, see our companion book for timeshare owners, **Winning the Timeshare Game - Making the Most of Your Timeshare**.

Buying to use vs. trade

There are different philosophies on buying timeshares.

Buying to use -- Most people buy at a resort (or in a vacation club) that they know they will enjoy. They are happy with the location and facilities, and their intention is to stay at that resort many times. They may exchange it for a different location some years, but they enjoy vacations at their home resort.

If you're buying to use your resort, a primary concern is how much you like your home resort, how well it meets the needs of your family, and whether you would all enjoy spending vacations there.

Buying to trade -- On the other side of the debate, some people buy a timeshare for the sole purpose of trading it. They could own it for years, without ever going near their home resort. Typically these people are knowledgeable and experienced timeshare owners.

If you're buying to trade, the primary concern is how much trading power this timeshare will give you, and how well it exchanges for the locations where you really want to stay.

Our recommendation -- Both approaches are valid, and have their supporters who are very happy and successful with them. However, if you are new to the world of timeshares, we recommend buying your first timeshare at a resort where you'd like to stay.

It can take time to figure out the ins and outs of timeshares, and exchanging is an area to explore and learn about before you put all your eggs in that basket. Whey you buy at a resort you know you'll be happy using, you know what you're getting. Exchanging introduces more uncertainty into the deal, especially when you're not used to working the exchange systems. Exchanges also increase your costs, since there are additional fees involved.

A wise approach is to first buy where you'd like to stay. Then you can move step by step into the area of exchanges, learning as you go.

Key question: How much do you like this place? -- If you can easily see your family vacationing at this resort year after year, that's an ideal scenario for buying a timeshare. Using your timeshare at your home resort is the most economical, since exchange fees add to the cost of swapping it for a different location. If you're buying with exchanges in mind, make sure to include that in your financial calculations.

Can you split your unit?

Most timeshares are resort condos, with studio, 1-bedroom, and 2-bedrooms being the most common unit sizes. If you buy a week in a 2-bedroom or larger unit, find out whether you can split your unit. This is a great advantage.

One common arrangement is to have a 2-bedroom unit with a lock-off (also called a lock-out). This has a locking door that can split the 2-bedroom unit into a 1-bedroom plus a studio. Both of these smaller units have their own kitchen, bath, and separate keyed entrance, so they can be used independently.

Why is this a good thing? Because it **gives you more options**.

* You can use the full 2BR unit for a week with your family.

* You can use a 1BR unit one week, plus a studio a different week, for 2 weeks of vacation.

* You can invite friends or in-laws for a vacation. They get the studio, you get the 1BR, and you each have enough facilities to stay out of each other's hair.

* You can use the studio week, and trade the 1BR for a week somewhere else.

* You can use the 1BR, and rent out the studio to help offset the maintenance fees.

If you're buying anything larger than a 1-bedroom unit, check into whether you can split it and use or trade the smaller units separately. It's quite a benefit when you can.

 Insider tip: Lock-off units in weeks vs. points -- The concept of lock-offs works a bit differently if you own weeks vs. points.

  * **Weeks**. If you own a week in a 2BR lock-off unit, then you can split it up into all the options as above. The studio and 1BR would both be for the season you own (high / mid / low).

  * **Points**. If you own points equivalent to a week in the same 2BR lock-off unit, then you could also use your points for a 1BR week + a studio week, but the calculations could work out a bit differently. You could use your points during different seasons, so that the cost in points of the 1BR + studio add up to either less or more than the original 2BR points.

 Insider tip: Splitting weeks for more trading power. If you own a week in a large lock-off unit, you can often get more trading power if you split your unit into two parts, and then deposit them separately with the exchange company. There are fees to do this, but it can make a big difference to what you can get.

Can you rent it out yourself?

Sometimes you can rent out your unit to a third party. This can be a good option to recoup some of your maintenance fee if you are unable to use your timeshare one year. The rules vary on what is allowed.

Renting usually allowed -- Usually you can rent out the specific week you own at a timeshare. Some resorts prohibit this though, which limits your options. Other resorts will allow you rent out your "home week" (the specific unit, season and week that you own), but not any other unit or week.

If you use points to book a stay at your own vacation club (i.e. not going through an exchange company), then you are usually allowed to rent that out, though you may need to pay for a guest certificate.

Renting not allowed -- If you exchange your home resort for a different resort, or purchase vacation time through one of the exchange companies like RCI or Interval International, then the rules prohibit you from renting this out to someone else. This includes exchanges and extra vacations - no renting allowed. These companies do enforce this rule, and you could lose both the money you paid and your membership if they find you breaking it.

Guest certificates -- Even though you can't rent out a unit you got via an exchange, you can buy a guest certificate that gives somebody else the ability to use your unit. This makes a fabulous gift - who wouldn't want to get a prepaid vacation? What you're not supposed to do is to take payment from somebody else for that gift.

Renting points -- This means selling someone the one-time use of your points, rather than selling them your points permanently. This is an alternative to booking a reservation with your points and then renting out that unit. The rules on renting points vary by company. In some points plans this is allowed with no problem. In other systems, like RCI points, you're allowed to give them away (transfer them) for free, but not sell them for money.

Rental rules and restrictions vary with different timeshare companies and resorts, so check the rules before you buy, so you know what your options are.

Consumer protections in the US and elsewhere

Most states in the US have regulations that apply to the timeshare industry, especially designed to protect consumers from high pressure sales. Specifics vary by state, but most places have a mandatory Rescission Period during which you can change your mind after purchasing a timeshare, and cancel the contract. This will probably not cover you if you buy a timeshare through a private resale contract rather than from a developer presentation. See the section *Timeshare rescission periods by US State*.

There are also rules about fraud and deceptive business practices that can protect you in case you were lied to or misled during the timeshare sales process. Once again, the specifics vary by state, but there is broad coverage in the country.

In Europe, the timeshare industry is regulated by certain European Directives (specifically 94/47/EC and 2008/122/EC), as well as national laws. Elsewhere in the world you may or may not have much in the way of consumer protection. Do your research beforehand so you know what risks you are taking.

If you purchase a timeshare with a credit card you can dispute the payment with your credit card company if there was a fraudulent transaction. If you buy a timeshare on eBay and pay with PayPal, you may be able to dispute it there, too.

Insider tip: Think about where to buy -- If you're considering a timeshare at some fabulous resort in an exotic destination that doesn't provide much for consumer protection laws, is that really a good idea? See if there's an associated resort in your home country/state, that provides better laws for consumer protection. It could be safer to buy a timeshare in your own country, and then just exchange or use your points to stay at that exotic resort.

6. Finances of Buying a Timeshare

This is not an investment

No matter what any timeshare salesman says, don't view a timeshare as an investment. This isn't like buying normal real estate, where the value typically appreciates over the long term. You cannot expect to get your money back when you sell a timeshare. In almost every case, the value goes down.

The more you pay, the more you stand to lose. If you're paying full retail price from a developer, then the value starts going down as soon as you sign the sales contract. If you pay tens of thousands of dollars for a timeshare, you could easily lose most of it when you resell your timeshare later.

If you buy a timeshare at a bargain price, then you can't lose that much, because you haven't put much into it. It's still not an investment, though, and don't buy thinking of this as a way to make money. There are a lot of bargain timeshares on the market, so you could have a difficult time unloading it for a profit. There are also fees to pay along the way - some related to buying and selling, and others like maintenance fees that have to be paid every year. Don't think of buying timeshares as an investment that will make you money.

 Insider tip: Imagine it gone -- Consider the cost of purchasing a timeshare as an expense, rather than an investment. If buying a timeshare is still a good deal, even when you consider the initial cost as a sunk cost, then go for it. If you're expecting to make money on the transaction, or even just get your money back after a few years, then it's probably not a good idea.

How much value will a timeshare hold?

It's a 99.9% probability that if you pay full retail price to buy a timeshare from a developer, the value will go down. What if you buy a lower priced resale timeshare? How much of your purchase price can you expect to get back if you keep it for 5 or 10 years, then want to sell it?

There are a number of factors that influence how much value your timeshare will hold over time.

* **How much you paid for it**. If you paid $500 for a timeshare, your chances of getting your money back are much greater than if you paid $50,000. If you paid $1, you could almost certainly sell it again for $1, though in difficult circumstances you might need to pay the closing costs.

* **Location, location, location**. Anytime you own a unit at a specific resort, location is a major factor in value. Everybody would love an ocean front unit in Maui, while the demand for Cornville, Arizona is considerably less.

* **Resort quality and upkeep**. Any expensive luxury timeshare could lose value, but a timeshare that's not maintained to the original standards will lose value even faster. You don't want to end up owning a 20-year old resort that looks like a faded remnant of its former glory.

* **Interval owned**. If you own a floating unit in low season (say November at a ski resort, when it's usually too cold to hike and too warm to ski), demand (and prices) will be low. High season slots will be worth more. Best of all are fixed weeks during peak season or major holidays. People will pay a premium to lock in vacation opportunities during these sought after time slots.

* **Competition**. What is the competition for your unit? If you own points or a floating week in a timeshare-saturated area with many comparable resorts, then you have a lot of competition and not much to differentiate your unit. If you own Christmas week at a unique timeshare with the perfect location at the bottom of the ski slope, then you have a lot less competition.

Key question: How special and unique is it? -- Do you own a beachfront unit where those are hard to come by? A fixed week over the Christmas holiday? The most luxurious resort along the coast? The more special and unique your timeshare is, the better your chances of getting something back when you sell it. If there are 30,000 other timeshare units in the area that are pretty much the same, don't count on getting back much of anything.

* **Contract expiration date**. Some right to use contracts expire after a designated period of time. The value of this goes down as it gets closer to the expiration date. If you have a timeshare contract that gives you the right to use a resort for the next 20 years, that's worth a lot more than a contract that's good for only 2 more years.

* **Resort buybacks**. Some resorts have a contract that gives them a Right of First Refusal if you resell the unit. Say you find a buyer willing to purchase your timeshare for $1,000. The resort company has the right to step in and buy it from you for $1,000 rather than letting your third party sale go through. Some companies have this right but don't exercise it, letting units go for $1 on eBay. Other companies actively buy back, to prevent anyone from buying their units so cheaply. This tends to keep the resale prices higher, but may not help you much as a seller. If the best offer you get on eBay is $50, then all the company has to pay you to exercise their right is $50.

* **The economy**. Just as a rising tide lifts all boats, a strong economy means a lot of people have more money to spend on vacations. The contrary is true, too. In a difficult economy people have enough problems covering their essential

expenses, and vacations are cut as a result. That means more bargain timeshares on the market, and lower prices overall.

* **Selling timeframe**. If you're not in a rush to sell your timeshare, then you can keep it on the market longer, waiting for a buyer who's willing to pay your price. If you need to get rid of it in a hurry, then you may need to accept a bargain basement price. This is when people sell their timeshares for $1, or even give them away.

Success Story - A timeshare that held its value

Use a timeshare for 9 years, then sell and get your money back

Wanting to escape the summer heat in Tucson with my family, I looked for options near San Diego. Hotels on the beach were very expensive, and could be booked up a year in advance for prime summer dates. A timeshare sounded like a good option, and the Carlsbad Inn seemed ideal.

There are very few timeshares on the beach in this area. The Carlsbad Inn is right across from the beach, and walking distance to the heart of the charming village of Carlsbad. Everything you want is right there.

Although the Carlsbad Inn had been built and sold out years earlier, there were some resale units offered by the resort. I wanted a fixed week in the summer, week 27, which often includes the fourth of July holiday.

There were no 2-bedrooms available, so I bought two 1-bedroom units just down the hall from each other, one for $10, 500. and the other for $13,000. (the more expensive one faced the inside grass area). This worked out even better than a two bedroom. The grown children stayed in the second unit and we each had our own privacy and space.

After enjoying these units for more than nine years I sold one on Redweek.com in March 2012 for $10,500, the same as I paid for it. I also had it listed with the resort's resale office. Two days after my sale the resort contacted me with a buyer for $14,000. I would have netted about a bit less ($9,800) that way, after deducting their 30% commission.

Key takeaways:

1) This timeshare held its resale value because it had a prime location, highly desirable fixed holiday week, and little competition in the area. It's both special and unique.

2) The person who bought it in 2012 got a better deal buying it from Redweek at $10,500 than if they had purchased the same unit from the resort at $14,000.

Does financing a timeshare make sense?

Does financing a timeshare purchase make sense? **The short answer is No.**

A timeshare is not a real estate investment like a home, which you can expect to increase in value over the years. Timeshares purchased at retail prices are sure to lose value, and usually end up reselling for a small fraction of the original developer price.

A timeshare also is not an income generating investment like a rental property. Even if you can rent it out you may not get enough to cover your annual maintenance fees. (This isn't always allowed - see *Can you rent it out yourself?* for more.) Some people who really know how to work the system do make money renting out timeshare units, but most people don't. Unless you're highly experienced, don't walk into this thinking you can rent it as a money maker.

If you are thinking of buying an expensive timeshare and financing it, then consider the following facts:

* **High cost** -- Interest payments will make your annual cost of ownership even higher than it would be otherwise. How much do all those payments and fees add up to every year? Compare this to the costs of vacationing with a budget priced resale timeshare, renting a

timeshare, or even staying in a hotel, and you will find that this makes for very expensive vacations.

* **High risk** -- If you lose your job and need to sell your timeshare, not only will you be selling it at a loss (almost certainly), but you could end up underwater - owing more money on your loan than you can get for selling your timeshare. That's the last thing you need if you hit a difficult time financially.

Insider tip: Don't buy now, and don't finance -- Don't let the developer at a timeshare presentation sell you anything at retail prices, and especially don't let them sell you on something that would require financing. It's smarter to buy a resale, pay a lower price, and avoid the financing.

Fees, fees, fees...

There are different categories of fees and add-on costs that are associated with timeshares. You need to know about these up-front, so you can figure them into your budget from the beginning.

Purchase-related costs

These are one-time charges you have to pay when you first buy a timeshare. The numbers will vary with each specific deal. Make sure you know up front what you'll have to pay before you finalize the deal.

Note: These purchase-related costs are generally only applicable when you buy a timeshare as a resale. If you buy a retail unit from the developer, you probably won't see these fees - they'll be covered by the exceedingly high price you pay.

* **Closing costs** -- This is money you pay to the title company that handles your closing. It may include escrow services as well. Typically $300-500.

* **Transfer fee** -- The resort company charges a fee to transfer the unit (or points) to a new owner. This could be $200 or more.

* **Title insurance** -- This is to protect you in case there are any problems with the seller's title to the unit. It's an optional charge - you choose if it's worthwhile for you. The typical cost could be $100 to $300 or more.

* **Recordation fee** -- If a deeded unit is recorded with a county clerk, there may be a recordation fee charged for this. This could be in the neighborhood of $50, depending on where you are.

* **Attorney fee** -- Some places require documents to be prepared by an attorney, which means an extra charge.

* **Government fees** -- In some locations the government may charge an additional fee to purchase a timeshare.

Insider tip: Negotiate the closing costs -- Sometimes a seller will be willing to pay part of the closing costs, or even all of them, if they're a highly motivated seller. If you negotiate this up front, it can lower your initial outlay for the purchase.

Recurring fees

Usually paid annually, these are the fees you need to pay over and over. This is the on-going obligation you take on when you buy the timeshare. You have to pay these fees whether you use your timeshare or not.

* **Maintenance fees** -- The cost of cleaning, managing, and maintaining the property is split between all of the owners, in the form of maintenance fees. Larger units, more deluxe resorts, and bigger points packages have higher maintenance fees. These fees are usually billed annually, though some places break them into monthly payments.

* **Property taxes** -- Taxes depend on what you own and where you own it. The property taxes are often built into your maintenance fees, but sometimes you'll see them broken out separately.

Insider tip: Itemized property taxes -- If property taxes are itemized on your bill, you may be able to count these on your tax return like other property taxes. Check with your accountant about your personal tax situation.

* **Club membership** -- If your timeshare purchase gets you a membership to a vacation club, check on the membership fees for the club. These may be rolled into the maintenance fee or broken out separately, but they can be significant ($200-300 per year).

Insider tip: Club fees can make a big impact -- Fixed club fees make it less attractive to buy a small number of points. If your base maintenance fee for a small package of points is $350, but the fixed club fee adds $299, that's a huge increase that almost doubles your annual cost. See if there's a way you can avoid joining the club, though you'll probably find it's mandatory. Remember that companies can (and do) raise these fees whenever they want. If you're locked in, there's nothing you can do about it.

* **Exchange membership** -- If you want to exchange your timeshare through RCI or Interval International, there is an annual membership fee. This covers you for a year, no matter how many exchanges you make during that time. The membership fee currently runs $84 to $124 per

year. In most cases this is optional, and if you don't anticipate trading then you don't need to pay it. Some timeshare companies automatically include a membership, so you don't have a choice in the matter.

Insider tip: Timing of fee payments --
Verify when you need to make fee payments vs. when the deal closes. You may encounter a situation where you're asked to pay maintenance fees between the date you initiate the purchase and the time the deal closes.

For example, you purchase a timeshare in December, with fees due Jan 1, and you're responsible for that year's maintenance fees. Your deal could still be somewhere in the closing process when the fees are due. It may be worrisome to hand over this extra money when you don't own the timeshare yet, but often the resort won't process the transfer unless the fees are current.

Usage fees

These are fees that you only pay when you use your timeshare, or exchange it and stay at a different property.

* **Exchange fees (weeks)** -- When you exchange your timeshare week for a stay at a different resort there is an exchange fee. Expect to pay about $199 per exchange.

* **Transaction fees (points)** -- When you use your points to book a stay at a resort there may be a transaction fee. The charge depends on how long you stay and how you book the reservation, but you could pay up to $159 for a 1-week stay.

* **Cancellation fees** -- If you make a booking and then later cancel it, you will probably be out a cancellation fee or lose the exchange fee that you paid. With RCI you can buy insurance to protect you in case you have to cancel, but then you're paying for the insurance.

* **Guest certificates** -- If you want to book a unit and let somebody else use it then you pay for a guest certificate.

Resort fees

Individual resorts may add on extra fees of their own. It's an unfortunate trend these days, with many airlines and hotels using various add-on fees to increase their revenues, and timeshare resorts are following along. Usually you shouldn't have to pay these fees to use a week you own at your home resort, but if you want to stay somewhere else, then watch for added fees like these.

* **Registration fees** -- Some resorts charge a flat registration fee to everyone when they arrive to check in to the resort.

* **Housekeeping fees** -- You'd think that housekeeping would be included in the cost of staying at a resort. Usually it is, but you'll find that some places charge an additional "housekeeping fee". This is most common when you're using points.

* **Resort fees** -- Just like hotels, some timeshare resorts now charge a daily "resort fee", that covers the use of the pool, exercise room, internet, and other facilities.

Alert: All inclusive fees -- Some resorts hit you with a mandatory all-inclusive fee, that covers all your food and drinks while you're there. It's a nice concept, but the fees can be huge, **up to $1000 per person** for a week's stay. If you thought you were getting a good deal on a vacation, this could completely change the equation.

Buying a timeshare at an all-inclusive resort can also negatively impact your trading power, since many people don't want to exchange where they'll have to pay steep all-inclusive fees. Make sure to double check this before you buy or book at any resort, especially in the Caribbean or Mexico, where this is quite common.

Special assessments

Special assessments are not normal or recurring expenses, and only happen occasionally. These are special costs for owners, to pay for major repairs or upgrades. This is over and above the regular annual maintenance fees.

How it works with weeks -- If your resort needs major repairs (for instance a roof replacement), beyond what can be covered with the normal maintenance fees, this cost will be billed to owners as a special assessment. The total cost is divided among the owners, proportionally based on how much they each own.

A special assessment might be a few hundred dollars, or even a few thousand in a rare worst case scenario. This one-time charge will show up on your annual bill, added to your normal maintenance fees. It's not something you want to receive. The only good thing about a special assessment is that unlike maintenance fees, you only have to pay it once.

Insider tip: Ask about special assessments -- Before you buy a bargain timeshare, check whether there are any pending assessments. That could be a nasty surprise!

Scam alert: Points owners don't get special assessments -- A common line used to convince weeks owners to "upgrade" to points, is to raise the threat of a special assessment, and say that changing to points will allow the owner to avoid that extra cost. This is not really true. Even if you own points, the timeshare owners will still pay for repairs at a resort. The developer isn't going to just swallow the cost - it's passed on to the owners.

How it works with points -- Say you own points in a resort group with 8 different resorts. If one of these resorts requires significant repairs or upgrades, the cost will be split among the points owners of the entire group of 8 resorts. This makes your share a lot less than if you were a direct owner of the one resort with a problem, with all costs split between owners of that single resort. On the other hand, it also means you share in the repairs for all 8 resorts, not just one, and may end up paying for repairs at resorts you'll never even see.

With points, you usually won't see these repairs itemized as a special assessment. Instead, the cost will just be rolled into your annual bill. When they say you won't pay special assessments, you'll still pay - it just won't be called a special assessment.

Alert: Low maintenance fees aren't always a good thing -- Once a timeshare resort is sold out, control passes from the developer to the resort's Home Owners' Association. Obviously, owners want to keep the fees low, but sometimes this can go too far. Deferred maintenance on a regular basis can mean higher costs later on. If you see a property with low fees that's looking a bit rundown, be aware that this could lead to a special assessment (or dramatic increases in maintenance fees) down the road.

Calculating the true cost of a timeshare

When you're looking at buying a timeshare, you need to know what the true cost of ownership will be. Some things like special assessments you can't forecast and hopefully won't see, but most costs are predictable, and you need to plan for them.

Initial purchase -- Up front, you need to pay the purchase price and associated closing costs.

* Purchase price
* Closing costs
* Transfer fee
* All other initial costs

Total up-front cost

Annual costs -- This is what you will spend each year that you own the timeshare. Your total will depend on whether you expect to stay at your home resort, or want to do an exchange.

Staying at home resort/club
* Annual fee (including maintenance fee, property taxes & club fee)

Exchanging to other resorts
* Annual fee (as above)
* Exchange company membership fee

   *   Exchange / transaction fee
   *   Resort add-on fees for non-owners

   Estimated annual costs

Example: Say you're buying a 1-week 1-bedroom resale timeshare for $2500, with $250 closing costs and $200 resort transfer fee. Your annual maintenance fee is $600. The resort is part of RCI, and you plan to stay at your home resort some years, and exchange to a different resort others.

Initial purchase	
Purchase price	$2,500
Closing costs	250
Transfer fee	200
Total up front costs	$2,950

Annual costs	No exchange	With exchange
Maintenance fee	$600	$600
RCI membership		89
Exchange fee		199
Resort add-on fees		100
Total annual costs	$600	$988

- Yearly cost (staying at your resort): $600
- Yearly cost (exchanging): $988

Insider tip: Save money at your own resort -- As you can see, the annual costs are significantly less if you stay at your home resort than if you exchange to stay somewhere else. If your goal is to take economical vacations, then it makes sense to buy at a location you'll enjoy.

What about the up-front costs? You can view the up-front purchase price different ways, but don't plan to make a profit on it. If you got a great deal on this timeshare to start with and it's a property that holds its value well, then you might be able to recoup your investment down the road when you decide to sell the timeshare. On the other hand, look around at the number of timeshares on sale for $1, and you'll see what can happen.

Key question: Would you sell it for $1? -- If you look at the purchase price as a sunk cost, and think about selling your timeshare for $1 when you're done with it, would you still make this transaction?

The answer can easily be yes. If you got a great deal on the purchase price, the up front cost can be negligible, or recouped in a year or two of economical vacations. Even paying thousands of dollars for the purchase can be worthwhile if it enables you to vacation in a special place with your family each year, in a way that would otherwise be difficult or impossible.

Key question: Can you cover the costs comfortably? -- The key word here is "comfortably". You don't want to get into a timeshare if it's too much of a stretch. Look at both the up front costs and the on-going annual costs, and make sure that both of these fit comfortably in your budget. Remember that annual maintenance costs generally rise.

It's best if you have some safety margin on this, in case of unexpected increases or additional costs. Perhaps the roof will start leaking, and require a special assessment for replacement. Do you have enough of a cushion financially so that you have a bit in reserve for an unexpected cost like this? If the standard costs are already maxing out your budget, then something like this popping up can be a problem.

7. How to Research a Timeshare Bargain

Doing your due diligence

When you're buying a timeshare through the resale market, you need to do some homework first, to make sure what you're getting. Some of the consumer protections for the timeshare market (like the automatic rescission period) may not apply when you seek out and buy a resale directly. You'll probably see phrases like "all sales are final".

Due diligence is when you investigate the facts about something before signing a contract. In the case of a timeshare, you want to investigate the property, the developer or management company, and the deal. If you check things out up front with a thorough due diligence you can end up with a winner, not a lemon.

 Insider tip: A few hours can save you a lot -- This due diligence process may seem like a lot of work to go through, but it really takes just a few hours, and it's well worth the effort. Make sure you know what you're doing so you don't get into a bad deal that could cost you in terms of money, frustrations, and future difficulties. The more you know going into a deal, the better your chances of ending up with a winner.

Insider tip: Ask questions before you bid -- When you're looking at timeshare bargains on eBay, be sure to ask all your questions before you bid on an auction. Even if you're still thinking it over, your bid may end up being the winning bid, which means you're committed to the purchase. The time to verify details is before you make a bid.

Research the property

With typical timeshare deals, you're buying into a specific resort. You can exchange it for time at a different place, but this is your home resort. Make sure the resort is a place that you would be happy to stay for vacation. If it's not a place you're happy, chances are that it won't give you a great exchange value either.

Here are some avenues to help you check out the property.

Rent at the resort -- If possible, this is ideal. Rent a night or two at the resort, in the type of unit that you'd like to buy, and you can get a first hand view of what it's really like. Try out the pool, the exercise room, the kitchen, and the restaurant. Take maximum advantage of this opportunity to explore and experience, and find out if it's really a place you'd be happy with. This isn't always practical, but it's a great method of discovery when you can do it.

 Insider tip: Renting through an exchange company -- If you already own a timeshare that's part of either RCI or Interval

International, then you may be able to arrange a stay at the resort you're thinking of through them. Look into visiting your target resort by either exchanging into it, using points to stay there, or buying extra vacation time. There's nothing like seeing a place in person to really know how you'd like it.

Walk through resorts -- If you're vacationing in an area that you would like to come back to, you can check out a few resorts while you're there. You don't need to sit through one of their sales presentations - a quick walk through and look around will give you a better feel for what the location and facilities are like. For instance, if you're at Lake Tahoe on vacation, take a quick look at a few resorts. That way if you see Lake Tahoe come up when you're looking at bargain timeshares later, you'll already have a few ideas about the resorts there.

Visit the resort website -- If you search online, you can usually find the resort's own website. Obviously this will show you the most positive view of the property, but it can be useful to see pictures, unit layouts, lists of amenities, etc. There's usually a page for Contact information if you want to call with more questions. If they rent units out directly there may be a Reservations page too, where you can find the room rates they charge to non-owners.

Check reviews on TripAdvisor -- This is one of the largest travel review sites on the web, and a good source. Do a Google search for *"tripadvisor reviews <u>resort name</u>"*.

Double check that it's giving you the precise property you want, since some timeshare resorts have an attached hotel, and others have very similar names. Read through the reviews and you'll usually discover a lot of interesting details about the property, facilities, and what's nearby. Read them with a critical eye, and try to separate common issues from one person's unique experience or viewpoint. *tripadvisor.com*

Check photos on TripAdvisor -- TripAdvisor has both Professional Photos (often the same as on the resort website) and Traveler Photos (submitted by anyone who visits the place). Check them both. Sometimes the difference can be illuminating.

Search Redweek for owner reviews -- You know what visitors think, now what about owners? Do a search on "*redweek reviews resort name*", to find out. You'll find reviews here from owners, as well as from people who exchanged their own timeshare to stay at this property. Either way, it's a timeshare insider's view of the property. Always take reviews with a grain of salt, since an owner who wants to rent out their property may submit an overly glowing review. An overall consensus is more valuable than one person's rant or rave. *redweek.com*

Check it out on TUG -- The Timeshare User's Group has reviews and forum postings about timeshare properties. Do a search on "*tug2 reviews resort name*" or "*tugbbs resort name*", and see what turns up. Some of the information isn't available unless you pay the $15/

year membership fee, but if you're serious about buying a timeshare, that's a very good investment. *tug2.net*

Talk to an owner -- If you can visit the property in person, you could try asking people you meet around the resort if they're owners, and what they think of the place. If you can't visit in person, you can post questions in the forums on Redweek or TUG, to find out what owners generally think about the place, or to get specific questions answered.

General internet search - Do an internet search for the resort name, and see what turns up. It may be nothing more than you've already seen on the sites above, or there could be something unexpected. It doesn't hurt to check!

Research the company

Google the company -- Do an internet search on the developer and/or management company, and see what you find. You'll probably find their corporate website, as well as news articles about the company, and other sites that mention them. See if there's anything negative or unexpected.

Check with the Better Business Bureau -- If the company is in the US or Canada, then see what the Better Business Bureau has to say about them. Even if the company is not BBB accredited, the site still gathers information on the company and consumer complaints. If the BBB has enough data, they will rate the business from A to F. Low scoring companies could be a problem. *bbb.org*

Check Ripoff Report for complaints -- People complain on this site about companies they feel have ripped them off, including timeshare companies. Search by company name, and you may find issues with deceptive timeshare presentations (no surprise there), excessive fees, difficulty in making exchanges, etc. If there are just a few of these, it may not be a real problem for your purchase, especially if they're focused on the behavior of timeshare salespeople (whom you are bypassing with our recommended approach). On the other hand, some companies will turn up hundreds of complaints. Red flag! *ripoffreport.com*

See what owners say about the company -- Check what people are saying on Redweek and TUG about the company, not just the specific resort. If they have issues and complaints about how the company operates, then this could be a problem. People complaining on Ripoff Report may be timeshare newbies who didn't really understand how things work. Redweek and TUG both have a lot of timeshare knowledgeable users, so you'll usually get more informed opinions.

Research the deal

Know exactly what you're getting -- For timeshare weeks, you will be purchasing a specific type of unit (Studio, 1BR, etc), with rights to use it a certain amount of time (typically one week per year, but not always), during certain times of year (fixed, float, high season, etc). Make sure you know these parameters.

If it's a Points purchase, then you need to validate exactly what those points will get you. For example, will 5,000 points cover a week in July at the beach resort you want, or not? What would the points get you at different places in different seasons?

Other aspects of the deal are less obvious. Is it a deeded or right to use contract? Has the seller already used the unit in the current year, or will you be able to vacation there this year?

Compare selling prices -- Shop around and see what other people are asking for the same thing. You may see the resort reselling a unit for $10,000, while Redweek has the same thing for $2,500, or eBay for $1,500. It pays to look around.

Compare maintenance fees -- While you're looking, see what maintenance fees are running on similar properties. You don't want to end up paying abnormally steep annual fees.

Insider tip: Annual fees are the key -- The initial purchase price is paid just once, but you're on the hook for the annual fees for as long as you own the timeshare. If the total annual costs don't work for your family vacation, then this isn't a good property for you. You are responsible for the annual maintenance fees each year, whether you use the property or not.

Insider tip: Look at fees per point -- When you're purchasing points in a vacation club, the maintenance fees per point can vary depending on which resort or resort group you're buying. It's meaningless to compare fees per point between companies (e.g. Marriott and Diamond points would be totally different). However, within a specific company, fees per point might vary between buying in the California group or the Hawaii group. It can pay to do a little comparison shopping and see where your annual costs per point are the lowest.

Check the seller -- If the seller is a company or a real estate agent, then check them out online to make sure they're reputable. If you're buying through eBay, then verify the seller's feedback score and transaction history. You want to see a feedback score of 100% positive, or very close to it. If the seller has a history of similar transactions, that gives them more credibility. On the other hand, you could find an individual selling their timeshare who has little or no eBay experience. It may still be a good deal, but you know less about them.

Verify ownership status -- Make sure that the seller owns this timeshare outright, with no unpaid financing, fees, or taxes. You can contact the resort directly to verify that the seller does in fact own the timeshare they say they do. Also ask whether the fees are up to date, or whether there is anything outstanding due. The resort won't always be willing to give you this information, but sometimes it works. If there's any question about the seller's title, then title insurance can protect you.

Verify all the fees -- Make sure you understand what additional fees will be due at the time of purchase, and later on too. Typically, up front you'll have to pay the purchase price + closing costs + a resort transfer fee. After the purchase you will need to pay recurring maintenance fees, club fees and taxes. Look beyond the sales price and make sure you understand all of the costs involved.

Run through your checklist -- A sample checklist is included at the back of this book, in the section *Timeshare Buyer's Checklist.* This includes a list of questions to ask and things to think about before you sign any contract to buy a timeshare. If your research so far hasn't provided the answers to any of these questions yet, then ask the seller, resort, or other owners for more information.

Red flags to avoid like the plague

If you find any of these issues then walk (or run!) away from this deal. While many aspects of a timeshare are personal and subjective (does the resort fit your style, or the deal fit your budget), the following are red flags to watch out for in any timeshare deal.

* **Too many complaints, especially post-sale** -- Pretty much every company will turn up some complaints against it, but some companies have hundreds of them. If most of the issues are with deceptive sales, it's a bad sign, but at least you're bypassing that part of the process. If there are a lot of post-sale complaints about either the resort or the developer, that's a definite red flag.

* **Property in a state of disrepair** -- If an older resort is getting rundown, this can be a problem, even if you get a bargain price and low maintenance fees. First of all, it won't get you much value for trades. Secondly, there's a distinct possibility of major repairs being required in the near future, leading to special assessments or steep fee increases.

* **Too many units for sale at bargain prices** -- Especially in a down economy, you will see timeshares for sale for as little as a dollar, or sometimes even for free. People lose their jobs, can't afford to keep up the payments, and want to

get rid of it in a hurry. However, you may find that there are an unusually high number of bargain basement sales from a particular resort. This can indicate a problem that's causing people to dump this property.

* **Unreasonable maintenance fees** -- Sometimes a property can end up with exceptionally high maintenance fees. Perhaps they got behind on maintenance and now have serious costs. Perhaps the management company is taking an outsized cut. Or perhaps enough units went to foreclosure that the maintenance burden is now split between a smaller number of owners. Whatever the reason, don't buy if the annual maintenance costs are too far out of line, compared with other similar resorts.

* **Pending special assessments** -- Sometimes large repair or upgrade projects are handled by charging owners a special assessment on top of the normal maintenance fee. Make sure there's nothing like this pending, or you could get an unpleasant surprise. You'd hate to pay $1 for a timeshare, then get a bill for a $3,000 special assessment!

* **Seller lacks credibility** -- If you're buying a resale from a company or real estate agent, then you can probably find some information about them on the web. If it's an eBay seller, check their feedback. If you're buying privately through

Redweek or other sources, or it's a new seller on eBay, you'll need to talk to the person to find out more. If you see negative feedback, or get any kind of bad feeling about the seller, then drop the deal.

* **No consumer protections** -- Different countries have different consumer protections in place for timeshare buyers and owners, and it's a good idea to research this if you're considering an international purchase. An alternative to buying in a country where you're not protected is to buy in a safer place, and then exchange for a vacation in that exotic destination.

Success Story - San Diego for $1

In August 2012, I purchased a Studio timeshare at the Gaslamp Plaza Suites in downtown San Diego, for $1 on eBay.

We had previously visited this resort, and loved the renovated historic building, the prime location in the Gaslamp district, and the rooftop patio. When I saw it for $1, I knew it was what I wanted.

I paid the seller's title company $299, which included the closing costs, transfer fee and clear title.

The maintenance fee for 2012 had already been paid, so I was getting a free week in 2012. By the time the deal closed, it was too late to book a week at this resort (the Gaslamp was full for the rest of the year), but I could still deposit the free week into RCI for a vacation elsewhere.

In this case, the resort HOA was also selling resale units, for $1,000 and up. By shopping on eBay, I was able to get the same thing for a lot less.

When using eBay, research your seller, check their feedback score and use PayPal through the eBay invoice system. This provides some degree of protection in case you encounter problems with the deal.

Key takeaways:

1) Shopping eBay for timeshares can give you some great bargains!

2) If you know a resort that you'd like to buy, you can watch eBay and other sources to see when one

8. Case Studies - Researching the Bargains

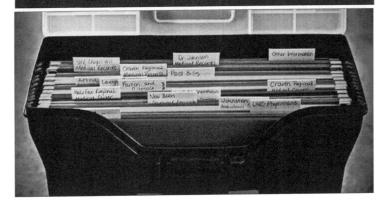

Case 1: A week for sale in Maui

The opportunity

Let's say you see a listing on eBay for a **week at the Maui Beach Vacation Club**, selling for $399. You'd love to vacation on Maui every year at a fabulous resort, so it sounds quite appealing. As much as you'd love to go check it out in person, that's just not feasible, so you need to do some research online. This case study will walk you through the steps.

Here's the original listing on eBay:

Checking out the resort

With a few quick Google searches, you turn up the following sites:

✱ Resort website --

Maui Beach Vacation Club resort site - *http://www.mauibeachvc.com/*

Of course this is going to show you the best side of the resort, but it does include photos, floor plans, a blog (with some useful info like upcoming changes to property taxes), and contact information for the resort itself. They also have a reservation system online for rentals, where you can see what you'd pay just to rent there at different time periods. So far, so good.

✱ Resort page on management company site --

http://www.crmlv.com/property_maui_beach.asp.

This doesn't tell you a whole lot about the property, but does give a list of amenities, shows floor plan diagrams, and tells you that it's part of both RCI and Interval International, so you would have a lot of trading flexibility.

✳ **Resort page on Interval International site** --
http://www.intervalworld.com/web/cs?
a=1503&resortCode=MBV

This doesn't give you much new information, but it does give you a bit more information including a map and a schedule of which months have the highest demand.

✳ **Traveler reviews on TripAdvisor** --
http://www.tripadvisor.com/Hotel_Review-g60632-
d813188-Reviews-Maui_Beach_Vacation_Club-
Kihei_Maui_Hawaii.html

You can read 40 reviews from people who stayed here, who rated it everywhere from Terrible to Excellent, with an average rating of 3.5 out of 5. You find out that it's right across the street from the beach, has no air conditioning in any of the units but they're usually OK thanks to the breeze, and that some people found it noisy. If you're looking for a 5-star resort, you can cross this off the list right now. On the other hand, if it seems like a possible fit for you, keep going.

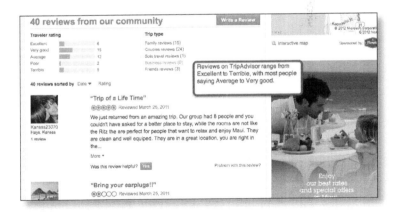

* **Owner reviews on Redweek** --
http://www.redweek.com/resort/P1188-maui-beach-vacation-club.
There are 15 reviews posted here, with average rating of 4 out of 5 stars. You'll also see if anybody has resales posted here. As on TripAdvisor, there are ratings across the spectrum. Some people remark that it's dated and small, while others are owners who have been coming here for years and adore it. It's not the Four Seasons, but you're looking at paying $399 for it, not thousands. Read through what people say, and see if you'd be happy or disappointed with this type of property.

* **Resort feedback on TUG (Timeshare User's Group)** --
*http://tug2.com/RnR/TabResortDescription.aspx?
Tab=D&ResortGUID=02d228c3-6322-4e3d-992d-40f4c09
6d288*
Here you can read more reviews, check out forum postings, and also see what people have for sale or rent at this resort. It seems that the units are quite basic but functional, and the resort is in a good location.

Key question: Will this resort fit your style? -- After you've read all the reviews, you need to make a decision about whether you'd be happy here. Would a simple, clean, convenient place to stay on Maui work for you, or do you really want something more luxurious? If it's not your style, then cross this resort off your list and keep looking.

Checking out the company

  * **Management company site** --

Soleil Management / Consolidated Resorts Management
website
http://www.crmlv.com
This gives you a little background on the company, as
well as info on which other properties they own, and
what associations they belong to. You can see they're
affiliated with both RCI and Interval International, and
that they're a member of the ARDA (American Resort
Development Association).

  * **Ripoff reports for Soleil Management** --

*http://www.ripoffreport.com/Search/Soleil
%20Management.aspx*
Here you find complaints from people who were duped at
timeshare presentations, sitting there for hours and
buying into the hard sell. That's why you don't play that

game, right? Also, there's somebody who says they got bills for maintenance fees every 3 months instead of once a year, and something about Consolidated Resorts entering bankruptcy in 2009.

  -- **Maintenance fees?** If the company really does engage in over-billing, you'd probably see something about that on Redweek or TUG. Since there's nothing there, it's most likely a misunderstanding or isolated billing problem.

  -- **Bankruptcy?** On further investigation, you find that Consolidated Resorts completed a chapter 7 bankruptcy in 2010, while the separate company Consolidated Resorts Management never entered bankruptcy. Operations are continuing as normal at their properties, so things are OK now.

Checking out the deal

  ✳ **Verify exactly what you're getting** --
This sale is for a 1BR unit, for an annual floating week that includes high season, so you should be able to use it almost any time of year (sometimes holiday weeks are separate). Your usage year would start in June 2013, and the contract has no expiration. A couple of things to check on:

  - Does your float include Christmas and New Year's? Any other exceptions?

  - Is it a deeded unit vs. right to use?

  ✳ **Check the seller** --

The seller has 100% positive feedback, with one other transaction that was a timeshare sale.

✳ **Check comparison prices** --

The price of this eBay deal is $399 right now. You can find the same thing on Redweek for $2500 and on TUG for $995, so this is the best deal at the moment. Maintenance fees are $720 per year, which is in line with other 1BR timeshares on Maui.

✳ **Verify all the fees** --

For closing you'd owe $350 closing costs + $200 resort transfer fee + $399 purchase price (if you won the bid at this price). That would be a total of $949 due on closing, if bidding doesn't raise the price. The annual maintenance of $720 would be due in June.

✳ **Rental price comparison** --

First year usage = $949 + $720 = $1669
Subsequent year's usage = $720 (if maintenance fees stay the same)

Rental prices (low season) = $139/night = $973
Rental prices (high season) = $232/night = $1624

The pricing looks like a good deal compared to rental costs (using rental prices from the resort's own website). Your first year (including the initial purchase costs) works out to about the same as rental prices in high season. After that, your annual cost is a bargain in comparison to renting for a week.

Conclusion?

Everything looks OK in your due diligence. There were no red flags turned up, and financially it makes sense. Now you can make an informed personal decision.

Key questions: How are you with the style and budget?
    * **Style** -- The resort is relatively small and simple, not a luxury property. Would you be happy staying here with your family?
    * **Budget** -- Taking all the costs into consideration, will it work for your budget? Make sure you leave a cushion in case you run into unexpected costs (timeshare related or other). You don't want to make this too much of a stretch.

As you look at other bargain timeshare deals, you can follow these same steps to investigate them and do your due diligence. With all the information that's available on the internet, it doesn't take more than a few hours to gather the information you need to make sure you end up with a winner, not a lemon.

Case 2: Vacation club points for sale

The opportunity

In browsing through the listings on eBay, you find this listing for **3500 points in the Shell Vacation Club**, available for only $1. Sounds like a deal, right? This case study will walk you through the steps to research and evaluate this opportunity, with a bit less detail than in case #1.

Checking out the resorts

In this case, you wouldn't be buying at a specific resort, you'd be buying points in the Shell Vacation Club, which has 24 resorts in North America According to the eBay posting, they have resorts in Hawaii, California, Arizona,

Nevada, North Carolina, Oregon, Wisconsin, Texas, New Hampshire, Canada and Mexico.

This means that rather than checking out a single resort, you need to research the resorts you could stay in with these points.
Here are the steps to follow:

1) See which of the club resorts look like places you'd like to go.
2) Check what 3500 points would get you at the resorts you like.
3) Dig into those selected resorts a bit further.

1) Where can you stay?
Shell Vacation Club website -
http://www.shellvacationsclub.com
On this site, you can browse through the resorts in this club. Many of the 24 locations don't appeal to you, but a couple of them that catch your eye are the Vino Bello Resort in Napa, CA, and the Kona Coast Resort, in Hawaii. These two both look appealing to you.

2) What can you get there with 3500 points?
Unfortunately, this isn't as easy to find as the resort descriptions, since Shell doesn't make this available on their public website. Fortunately, if you Google "*Shell vacation club points chart*", you can turn up a copy of the Shell points chart on a different site.

Here's what you find for your selected resorts.

Vino Bello Resort

Season	Unit	Fri-Sat	Thu, Sun	Mon-Wed	Week
Platinum	Studio	650	450	350	3250
Platinum	1BR	1200	800	600	5800
Platinum	2BR	1850	1250	950	9050
Gold	Studio	600	400	250	2750
Gold	1BR	1150	750	450	5150
Gold	2BR	1750	1150	700	7900
Silver	Studio	500	350	200	2300
Silver	1BR	950	650	400	4400
Silver	2BR	1450	1000	600	6700

3500 points at Vino Bello would get you

* **Studio** for a week any time of year (2300-3250 points).
* **1BR** for up to 5 week nights in any season (without Fri or Sat nights)
* **2BR** for a weekend (Fri+Sat) in Silver or Gold seasons, or a few non-weekend nights

Kona Coast Resort

Season	Unit	Fri-Sat	Thu, Sun	Mon-Wed	Week
Platinum	1BR	800	750	550	4750
Platinum	2BR	1100	950	750	6350
Platinum	3BR	1450	1300	1000	8500
Gold	1BR	700	650	500	4200
Gold	2BR	1000	900	700	5900
Gold	3BR	1350	1200	950	7950

3500 points at Kona Coast would get you

* **1BR** for 4-5 nights in Platinum season or 4-6 nights in Gold season

* **2BR** for 3-4 nights in Platinum, or 3-5 nights in Gold
* You couldn't get a full week in any season or unit type

Key question: Would what you can get fit your needs? -- This depends on your personal situation. If you're traveling with a family and need a 2BR, then chances are this won't get you enough time, with just a weekend in Napa or 3-5 nights in Kona. Flying to Hawaii for 3-5 nights isn't very cost effective. If you're traveling as a couple, where a studio or 1BR would fit your needs, then these points could make more sense.

* **Resort reviews (TripAdvisor, Redweek, & TUG)**
You search all three sites for reviews on the two resorts, and here's a quick summary of what you find.

* **Vino Bello Resort** --
TripAdvisor has mostly excellent reviews (4/5 average), with a few others mixed in. It sounds like a nice place with spacious units, but not in the most convenient or charming location. Redweek reviewers give it 4/5, and it sounds like the units are nice, but it's in a corporate park rather than in town or in the vineyards. TUG reviewers give it 8.7/10 Most people there were quite happy with it, though the studios didn't have a stove (just a microwave), and some units face the parking lot. Overall, it seems quite positive, unless you're picturing a charming little place surrounded by vines.

✳ **Kona Coast Resort** --

Once again, TripAdvisor shows mostly excellent reviews (4.5/5), and a lot of people are delighted here. One review worth noting was from a longtime owner there, who was disappointed that things were looking worn out, and wondered about the maintenance fees they paid. Redweek reviewers give it 4.5/5, and the reviews from 2008-09 talked about renovation work going on then. TUG reviewers give it 8.1/10, with many positive comments about the units. Negative notes were that most units face the golf course or parking lot (few ocean views), air conditioning costs extra, and if you take your towel to the beach and it comes back sandy, they charge you $20.

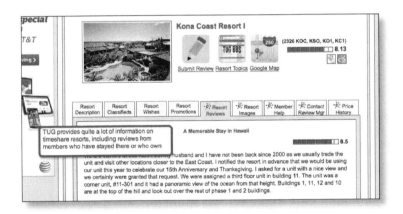

Key question: Would these resorts fit your style? -- After you've read all the reviews, it comes down to a personal decision about whether these resorts are what you'd want.

Would you be happy here? Would you want to spend some of your annual vacation time in these places?

Checking out the company

Searching for Shell Vacation Club didn't turn up any red flags, but it does show that the **company was bought by Wyndham** in Sept 2012.
http://www.shellvacationsclub.com/club/membernews.jsp

The official statement from Shell is that nothing will change for their members. In the short term that's probably true, though it's impossible to say what changes might occur in the long term with Wyndham now running the show.

Checking out the deal

  * **Verify exactly what you're getting** --
This sale is for 3500 points in the Shell Vacation Club. All fees are paid for 2013, so you'll owe annual fees of $829, not payable until 1/1/2014.
You get to use these 3500 points annually, starting 7/1/2013, so you could get a bargain on a 2013 vacation, since the annual fees were already paid by the seller. Shell does not allow the SVC Elite program or SVC Lifestyles to be used on resale purchases, but that doesn't matter - you're interested in the timeshare vacation opportunity.

✳ **Check comparison prices** --
The price of this eBay deal is $1 right now, and there are some other Shell points packages out there that are very cheap, also. On Redweek, there are more points packages, ranging from $1 to $20,000.

✳ **Check the seller** --
The seller has sold over 1,000 timeshares on eBay, with 100% positive feedback. That's an excellent sign.

✳ **Verify all the fees** --
In this case, the seller pays closing costs, and all you need to pay is the bid ($1) + the resort transfer fee ($200), for a total due at closing of $201. The seller uses a bonded escrow service (paid for) and guarantees clear title (no additional title insurance).

Annual maintenance fees (including Shell club + Interval International memberships) = $829. These have already been paid for 2013, will be next due on Jan 1, 2014.

✳ **Rental price comparison** --
First year usage = $0 maintenance (already paid) + $201 (at closing) = $201
Subsequent year's usage = $829 (if maintenance fees stay the same)

For price comparisons, you need to pick specifics to check. You can then check them against the company's own rental site, *www.shellhospitality.com.*

✻ **Vino Bello** -
Studio for full week, Platinum season (3250 points).
Cost with ownership = $829 (annual fees, after the first year)

Rental for a week in June = $293/night + taxes + fees = $2480 total

> You spend $829 for something that rents for $2480? Great deal!

✻ **Kona Coast Resort** -
1BR for 6 nights (Sat-Thurs), Gold season (3500 points)
Cost with ownership = $829 (annual fees)

Rental for 6 nights in June (Sat-Fri) = $104/night + taxes + fees = $705 total

> You spend $829 for something that rents for $705? Loser deal.

Conclusion?

The Shell resorts get generally high reviews, and most people seem to be happy with them, though there are a few drawbacks to consider. The company and seller are both reputable. The company was recently bought, but the official word is that nothing is changing. The seller is paying closing costs, and the price is just $1, so it's a low fee to get in.

Key question: Is it worth it? -- Perhaps, but you really need to give this some thought. The biggest question area is the annual maintenance fee, and how you'd use the unit.

* To stay in a studio in Napa, it's a great deal. Your points would be enough to stay for a week any time of year, at a much lower cost than you'd pay to rent the same thing.

* If you want to stay in Kona, it's a very poor deal. In Kona, you can't get a full week with your points, and it's cheaper just to rent than to use the points. If this is what you where you'd like to go, then just rent. You'll pay less and also avoid the on-going financial obligation.

Are there other Shell resorts that look appealing? You can follow the same process to check them out, too. In the end, it comes down to whether those points will get you enough benefit at places you'd like to go, to be worth the annual costs.

9. Putting It All Together

What's your next step?

Now that you've read the book, what do you think?

* Does the timeshare lifestyle seem like it would be a good fit for you and your family?

* Can you see yourself enjoying frequent vacations at a resort of your choice?

* Do you have a grasp of the different aspects of timeshare ownership?

* Would you like to save a lot of money by buying a timeshare bargain?

Recommended next step: Try a few "trial runs"

Before before you actually put your money on the table and buy a timeshare, it's smart to practice first. Try the whole system out - everything except the part about actually buying. You'll learn a lot when you do this!

1) **Pick your targets**. Choose 4 or 5 different bargain timeshares that look promising, from eBay or other online sites.

2) **Check them out**. Run each of your prospective deals through a full due diligence process, filling out the *Timeshare Buyer's Checklist* near the back of this book for each one.

3) **Research "as if"**. Go through the evaluation process as if you were really considering buying, but don't buy any of these. Right now, these are just for practice. You're furthering your education before you spend any money.

Insider tip: Practice, practice -- This process can be quite eye-opening. As you go through evaluating your trial run properties, you'll start to get a better feel for what's available, and what to watch out for. You'll also gain confidence in your own abilities.

Each time you do one of these practice runs, you'll learn a little more, and it will all become easier and faster. You'll also start to identify companies you are or aren't interested in, which will make it faster to weed through deals you see offered.

Yes, it takes time to do this, but the knowledge you gain can make an enormous difference in your outcome when you finally purchase a timeshare. You'll be able to find the deals, avoid the scams, and save thousands. Investing this time in your own education prepares you for *Winning the Timeshare Game*.

Read this book, practice the techniques, and dive in
when you're ready. You can do it!

10. Additional Resources

Timeshare glossary

Accommodation certificate (AC): A credit you get that is good for a stay at a resort. Interval International members may receive an AC good at specific resorts, during a specific timeframe. No timeshare exchange is required, just a reservation fee.

Accelerated use: A right to use program which allows a timeshare owner to use their vacation time more rapidly than normal. For instance, if you would normally have annual usage, you could take two or more vacations in a year rather than waiting until they'd normally be available.

Accrued weeks: Weeks that you carried over from a prior year, which are available for use during the current year.

Affiliated resort: Most timeshare resorts are part of a group of affiliated resorts, often built by the same developer or part of the same vacation club. Owners at one resort have preferential rights to use other affiliated resorts in the group.

All inclusive (AI): All inclusive resorts charge you a certain amount per person that covers all of your food, beverages, and activities while you stay there. Some places this is mandatory, other places it's optional.

Annual: With an annual timeshare, you have the right to use your timeshare every year. This is the most common arrangement.

ARDA (American Resort Development Association): A trade association for the US timeshare industry, which lobbies for policies that support the industry.

Bank: If you choose not to use your timeshare at your home resort, you can bank it with one of the exchange companies. You then have this available as a credit to exchange for a stay at a different resort.

Biennial: You have the right to use the resort every other year, as opposed to Annual, where you can use the resort every year. Also called Every other year (EOY), Even years, or Odd years.

Bonus time: Buying extra nights at your home resort, when space is available, at preferential owner rates.

BR: Short for bedroom. Timeshare units are usually either Hotel (no kitchen), Studio (one room with bed, sitting area and kitchenette), 1BR (one bedroom, separate living room and kitchen), or 2BR (two bedrooms, separate living room and kitchen).

Check in date: The most typical arrangement for timeshares is a 7-day stay. Some resorts offer Saturday to Saturday, others will have Friday to Friday, Sunday to Sunday, or sometimes a different day. If you have a

Saturday to Saturday week, then your check-in date is Saturday, even if you don't show up until Monday.

Closing costs: When you buy a timeshare there are typically certain costs associated with closing the deal. This can include deed preparation, recording fee, escrow fee, transfer fee, and administrative charges.

Club membership / Trust membership: A type of timeshare system where rather than owning a portion of a resort directly, you buy a membership to a club. The resort facilities are controlled by trustees, and your membership gives you a right to use the resort. Sometimes the trust is backed by deeds, sometimes not.

Cooling off period: Also called a Rescission period, this is a legally mandated time period during which you can change your mind after buying a timeshare. It's designed to protect consumers who are pressured into making a bad purchase. The length of time you have to rescind your contract varies from place to place, depending on local laws.

DAE (Dial An Exchange): An independent timeshare exchange company.

Deed: A legal document that proves ownership of a property. If you own a home or other piece of real estate, you have a deed to the property.

Deeded property: A piece of real estate with a deed that establishes the ownership. With a deeded timeshare, you have a deed to the specific property you own, typically one week per year in a certain type of unit. The deed is recorded with the appropriate government agency. Just like owning other real estate, you can sell it, rent it, or leave it for your heirs. Also called Fee simple.

Deeded trust: A vacation club where the trustees hold deeds to the property. The timeshare owners don't own a portion of the resort, instead they own a portion of the trust and a membership in the club, which gives them the right to use the resort. Not all vacation clubs have deeded trusts - some are not backed by deeds.

Destination club: Another term for Vacation club.

DVC: Disney Vacation Club.

EOY (Every Other Year): A timeshare that gives you the right to use the unit every other year. Same as Biennial.

Escrow: A secure system for arranging real estate purchases, where a trusted third party holds the buyer's funds during the closing period. Once the paperwork is done and the sale is finalized, the funds are released from escrow to the seller.

Exchange: Trading your timeshare at the resort you own, for a vacation at a different resort. There are several timeshare exchange companies that facilitate these exchanges.

Exchange company / Exchange network: A company which allows individual timeshare owners to deposit (or bank) their timeshare, making it available for exchange with other timeshare owners at different resorts. The largest exchange companies are RCI and Interval International.

Exchange fee: A transaction fee that you pay for processing a timeshare exchange.

Fee simple: Another term for deeded ownership, in which the timeshare owner actually has a deed to the property.

Fixed unit: A form of timeshare ownership where you own a specific unit at the resort, for a specific time period each year. For instance, you might own a week in unit #1714, and when you visit your resort each year, you always get that same unit.

Fixed week: A type of timeshare ownership where you own a specific week of the year at your resort. Typically the weeks are numbered starting with 1 at the start of the year. If you own week 19, then you get to use your timeshare the 19th week of each year. This could be combined with a fixed unit (e.g. you get unit #1714 the 19th week of each year), or it could be a certain type of unit (e.g. you get a 2-bedroom unit the 19th week of each year).

Floating: With a floating timeshare, you don't own a specific week at a resort, you own an interval of use that can float from week to week each year. At most resorts, the year is split into high, medium and low seasons, depending on demand. Owners purchase a floating week in a particular season. For example, you own a floating week in high season, which you can schedule anytime within that season. It's subject to availability, since you're competing for a given week with other owners who bought the same season. Some places consider the entire year to be high season, so your week can float throughout the year.

Fractional ownership: A timeshare arrangement where you own a fraction of a vacation property. Typically this term is applied in cases where you own more than one week per year at a resort.

Guest certificate: If you want to let someone else use your timeshare, or time that you purchased or exchanged at a different resort, you can do this by getting them a guest certificate from the resort or exchange company.

HGVC: Hilton Grand Vacation Club.

Holiday club: Another term for Vacation club.

Holiday ownership: Another term for timeshare ownership.

Home group: This is the group of resorts affiliated with your home resort. For instance, if you own a VRI timeshare, your home group includes a list of other VRI resorts. Usually, you get preferential booking rights within your home group.

Home Owners' Association (HOA): With deeded timeshares, the resort ends up being owned by all of the individual timeshare owners. The Home Owners' Association is responsible for decisions about how to run the resort, and owners have a right to elect the board of directors and vote on important issues. Typically the HOA contracts with a management company that handles the day to day operations.

Home resort: Usually (with the exception of some vacation clubs), your timeshare is purchased for a specific home resort. If you have a deeded timeshare, this is the resort listed on the deed. Your timeshare lets you stay at your home resort with no exchange necessary. Usually you have preferential rights at your home resort, such as the ability to make reservations earlier than other people.

Interval: A period of time for which you own a timeshare. The most typical interval is one week per year. This can be further narrowed to a specific interval, such as week 35. The dates for each week are defined on the resort's interval calendar.

Interval calendar: A yearly calendar which shows when each week starts and ends. For example, if a resort counts their weeks Saturday to Saturday (the day of week varies by resort), then week 1 begins on the first Saturday of the year, week 2 on the second Saturday, etc. Normally the year would include 52 weeks, but on years with 53 Saturdays, you end up with 53 weeks.

Interval International (II): The second largest timeshare exchange company, with thousands of affiliated resorts worldwide.

Lease / Leasehold: Rather than owning property outright, there is a long term lease to the property, and you purchase the right to use your timeshare during that time. Whereas a deeded property is yours forever, a lease has an expiration date. For instance, you might have a right to use lease contract which expires after 25 years. In some states and countries deeded ownership is not allowed, so timeshares are all handled as leaseholds.

Levy: A levy is a fee that you need to pay. This could be an annual fee, or a special charge to cover major costs. See Special assessment.

Lock-off / Lock-out unit: A large timeshare unit which can be split into separate pieces, and used, rented, or exchanged individually. For instance, a 2-bedroom unit that could be split into a 1-bedroom unit + a studio unit, each of which has its own kitchen and bathroom facilities, and its own keyed external entrance. Owning a lock-off unit provides the owner with greater flexibility on how to use it.

Maintenance fee (MF): When you buy a timeshare, you are responsible for paying an annual maintenance fee, which covers cleaning, maintenance, repairs, and management of the resort. The total cost of these items is split between all of the timeshare owners, and you receive an annual bill for your portion. Property taxes or club membership fees may also be bundled into the maintenance fee.

Management company: The management company is paid to handle the daily operation of the resort. Often, this is a company affiliated with the developer.

Maximum occupancy / Private occupancy: Each timeshare unit has a maximum number of people who can stay there. If you see a unit labeled "Occupancy 4 / 2", that means the maximum occupancy is 4 people, the private occupancy (in a closed bedroom) is 2 people, and the other 2 are non-private, typically on a pull-out sofa.

MVCI: Marriott Vacation Club International.

Points: A system of timeshare ownership where rather than owning a week at a specific resort, you buy a number of points. You can then spend these points to get vacation time at various resorts in the same points system. You're not tied to a 7-night stay. Your points might buy you 10 nights at a lower priced resort, or 5 nights at a higher priced resort.

Points for deposit (PFD): RCI's program where you can deposit a timeshare week into your RCI points account instead the normal RCI weeks account.

RCI (Resort Condominiums International): RCI is the largest timeshare exchange company in the world, with over 4,000 resorts in 100 countries.

Red week: Companies often use color coding to signify which weeks of the year are high, medium, or low season. Different companies use different color schemes, but red is a common designation for high season, so a red week is a week during the prime season at that resort.

Resale: If you buy a resale timeshare, you are buying a previously owned timeshare. The first owner buys a timeshare directly from the developer. When they sell it to the next owner, it becomes a resale.

Rescission period: Also called a Cooling off period. This is a legally mandated period during which you can change your mind about a timeshare purchase you made. The intent is to protect consumers from high pressure sales tactics which are common in timeshare presentations. The number of days varies by country and state. You can cancel (rescind) your contract during that time period with no financial impact.

Right to use (RTU): With a right to use timeshare, you don't actually have any deeded ownership in the resort. Instead, you have a contract that gives you a right to use the resort for a specific amount of time each year. This type of contract can have an expiration date, unlike a deeded unit.

Season: Most resorts divide the year into different seasons, depending on the demand for each season. At a ski resort, winter months may be high season, while at a beach resort, the summer months are high season. It costs you more to buy, rent, or exchange for a resort during high season than low season. Often there are color codes for the seasons, which can vary by company.

SFX: San Francisco Exchange, an independent timeshare exchange company.

Special assessment: When a resort needs major repairs or upgrades that aren't covered by the annual maintenance fees, the additional costs may be billed to the resort owners as a special assessment. This is a charge that's over and above your normal annual fees.

SVC: Shell Vacation Club.

SVN: Starwood Vacation Network.

Timeshare: A system of vacation ownership in which you own the right to use a portion of a vacation resort for a portion of the year. A typical arrangement is owning one week per year, in a certain type of unit, at a certain resort. Depending on the system, you may actually own a portion of the resort (a deeded timeshare), or you may just own the right to use the unit. Some timeshare systems sell you points rather than a fixed interval, and then you exchange your points for a stay at a resort.

Trading power: When you deposit your timeshare with an exchange company, it has a certain trading power based on the location, resort, unit type, week, and how far in advance you deposit it. Your possible exchanges are limited to other units that have equal or lesser trading power compared with what you have.

Trading Power Unit (TPU): A measurement used by RCI when exchanging units at one resort for another. You'll see it called Trading Power, or abbreviated to TPU. When you deposit your timeshare with RCI, you receive a certain number of TPU's for it, which vary depending on how desirable your resort, unit and time period are. You can then exchange for other timeshares which require the same number of TPU's or less.

Triennial: You have the rights to use the resort every third year, as opposed to Annual, where you can use the resort every year.

TUG (Timeshare Users' Group): An online site with a forum where timeshare owners share information. Members are sometimes referred to as tuggers.

Undivided interest (UDI): In some systems, you purchase an undivided interest in a property. Rather than owning a specific unit or a specific week, you own a non-specific small percentage of the property.

Vacation club: A type of timeshare system where rather than owning a portion of a resort directly, you buy a membership to a club. The resort facilities are controlled by trustees, and your membership gives you a right to use the resort. Sometimes the trust is backed by deeds, sometimes not.

Vacation ownership: Another term for timeshare ownership.

Vacation ownership interval (VOI): The period of time you own, typically one week per year of timeshare ownership.

WM: Worldmark Vacation Club.

Organizations and resources

Timeshare industry organizations

ARDA (American Resort Development Association) -- (US) A national organization for the US timeshare industry, which advocates for policies that promote the growth of the industry. *arda.org*

ATHOC (Australian Timeshare and Holiday Ownership Council) -- (Australia) This organization represents the timeshare industry in Australia, and works to promote industry practices. They also offer information and support to timeshare owners. *athoc.com.au*

CRDA (Canadian Resort Development Association) -- (Canada) The national organization in Canada, created to encourage and maintain a high standard of ethical conduct throughout the industry. Works with the ARDA on various initiatives. *crda.com*

OTE (Organization for Timeshare in Europe) -- (Europe) A trade association for timeshares in Europe, similar to the ARDA but with more focus on consumer affairs. The name has been changed to RDO (Resort Development Organisation). *rdo.org*

ROC (Resort Owners' Coalition) -- (US) Affiliated with the ARDA, this is an alliance of over a million timeshare owners, developers and managers. They propose and support legislative and regulatory policies. If you own a timeshare in the US, you can expect to see a "voluntary contribution" to this organization added to your yearly bill. *arda-roc.org*

RDO (Resort Development Organisation) -- (Europe) The trade association for vacation ownership across Europe, made of up of developers, exchange and management companies, and more. The purpose is to promote vacation ownership, protect the interests of the timeshare industry and owners, and target fraudulent activity that harms timeshare owners. Formerly called the OTE (Organisation for Timeshare in Europe). *rdo.org*

TATOC (The Association of Timeshare Owners Committees) -- (Europe) Run by timeshare owners for timeshare owners, this organization was created to safeguard and enhance the timeshare holiday experience for existing and prospective users, and be the voice of owners. The largest consumer association for timeshare owners in Europe, they have a consumer help line to aid in problem situations. *tatoc.co.uk*

Timeshare exchange companies

DAE (Dial An Exchange) -- Worldwide independent timeshare exchange company, not affiliated with specific resorts like RCI or II. Free membership. *daelive.com*

Interval International -- The second largest timeshare exchange network, with thousands of resorts worldwide. To use this, your timeshare resort must be affiliated with Interval International. Paid membership. *intervalworld.com*

Platinum Interchange -- Independent timeshare exchange company, not affiliated with specific resorts like RCI or II. The third largest timeshare exchange company. Free membership. *platinuminterchange.com*

RCI (Resort Condominiums International) -- The largest timeshare exchange company, with over 4,000 resorts around the world. To use this, your timeshare resort must be affiliated with RCI. Paid membership. *rci.com*

SFX Preferred Resorts -- Independent timeshare exchange company, specializing in highly rated resorts. Free or paid memberships. *sfx-resorts.com*

Timeshare Juice -- Site that lets you exchange your timeshare directly with other owners. Free membership. *timesharejuice.com*

Trading Places International -- Independent timeshare exchange company. Exchange for another resort, or apply your week toward a cruise. Free or paid memberships. *tradingplaces.com*

Vacation Point Exchange -- An online forum for people to exchange timeshare points in different companies (Disney, Marriott, and others). Free membership. *vacationpointexchange.com*

Useful websites

BBB (Better Business Bureau) -- A resource in the US and Canada that provides objective information on businesses. You can search for a company and find out their standing, as well as what consumer complaints have been filed against them. *bbb.org*

eBay -- An online auction site where people sell everything under the sun, including timeshares. This can be a good place to look for bargains. *ebay.com*

Redweek -- A site focused on timeshare sales and rentals. Owners can post their own timeshares for sale or rent, and potential buyers or renters can connect with them directly, with no middlemen or commissions. The site also provides resort reviews, a blog, and a forum. Basic membership is free, or you can pay $14.99/year for expanded access. *redweek.com*

Ripoff Report -- A site where consumers can file complaints against businesses they feel have ripped them off. You can search it to see what problems other people have had with a company, or to file your own complaint. This site tends to have more rants than the BBB, but it can be useful. *ripoffreport.com*

TUG (Timeshare Users' Group) -- An online user's group for people who own, or are thinking of buying, timeshares. There's a very active forum, which provides a wealth of useful information. The $15/year membership fee is well worth it if you're active (or want to become active) in timeshares. *tug2.net*

Timeshare rescission periods by US state

Most states in the US have mandatory rescission periods for timeshare purchases. Also known as "cooling off periods", these laws are designed to protect consumers who are the victims of high pressure timeshare sales.

The way it works is that you have a certain number of days to cancel (rescind) your contract if you change your mind. This can be a godsend for people who are pressured into buying something they don't want or can't afford.

If you have signed a contract to buy a timeshare, this rescission period gives you a little time to double check your finances, do further research on any aspect you're not sure about, or talk it over with your family. If you decide this is not a good deal for you then this is your opportunity to get out of your contract.

> **Note:** You must rescind your contract within the specified number of days or you lose your chance to do so.

The ARDA maintains a chart showing the rescission periods in different states. Some states have no mandatory rescission period, so as soon as you sign the contract, you have no easy way to get out of it. Most states allow at least 5 days.

When you refer to this chart, be sure to note that some states specify the length of the rescission period in business days, while others use calendar days.

Rescission periods by state:
http://www.arda.org/uploadedFiles/ARDA/
Government_Affairs/
Government_Affairs_Call_Out_Boxes/
RescissionPeriodsNov2010.pdf

If you are in a situation where you want to rescind a timeshare purchase, check directly with the state real estate board in the property state, to ensure that you have the most current information on their rescission period. If any state makes changes to this, there could be a lag between the legislative changes and updates on the ARDA site.

Note: Rescission periods normally apply only to timeshares purchased from the developer directly, not to timeshares you purchase on the resale market. The intent is to protect you from high pressure sales, which isn't applicable if you seek out a bargain timeshare yourself.

Timeshare buyer's checklist

Here's a checklist you can use to organize your research results when you're shopping for a timeshare bargain. If you're looking at multiple possibilities, print one copy of this list for each timeshare you're considering, so you can easily make comparisons.

For more detail on any of these items, see the appropriate section in this book.

You can also download a convenient printable version of this checklist from our website:

http://timesharegame.com/buyers-checklist

Winning the Timeshare Game - Buyer's Checklist	
Type of ownership	
Deeded or Right to use?	
Vacation club: Deeded trust or Non-deeded?	
Expiration date?	
Buying weeks	
Fixed or floating?	
Season - When can / can't you use it?	
Unit size and type?	
Can you split the unit (lock-off)?	
Buying points	
Where can you use the points?	
What can you get with that many points? (Need to see the points chart)	
The resort	
Where is the home resort?	

Winning the Timeshare Game - Buyer's Checklist	
What do the reviews say about it?	
Does it seem like a place you'd like?	
Are you allowed to rent it out?	
Where can you exchange (RCI, II, other?)	
Large number of bargain units for sale?	
The company	
What is the company's reputation?	
Are other owners happy with them?	
The financials	
Sales price	
Comparison prices for same resort/points	
Total closing / transfer costs	
Total due at closing	
Annual maintenance fees	

Winning the Timeshare Game - Buyer's Checklist	
Property taxes? Club fees?	
Total annual payments	
How do annual payments compare to renting at a comparable place?	
Any pending special assessments?	
Other aspects of the deal	
When can you first use it?	
When is the maintenance fee due?	
How credible is the seller?	
Likelihood of holding value? (See factors listed in book)	
If you sold it for $1 five years from now, would you still be happy with the deal?	

Want more advice?

1) **Free tips on website** -- Visit our website *TimeshareGame.com*, where we regularly publish timeshare tips, tricks, and deals. It's useful, it's easy, and it's free.

2) **Free newsletter** -- Subscribe to our newsletter, and we'll deliver timeshare tips, news, and insights to your e-mail, for free! Use the signup box on the website. We won't spam you or sell your contact details - it's just a way to send you useful timeshare information.

3) **Personal consultation** -- Do you have specific questions you'd like to discuss with us? Ask about a personal consultation. If you're interested, e-mail a brief summary of your situation to *info@timesharegame.com*, to see if it's something we can help you with. Please note that we are not lawyers, and cannot provide legal advice.

4) **Owner's guide** -- Once you own a timeshare, you'll want to check out our companion book for owners, ***Winning the Timeshare Game: Making the Most of Your Timeshare***. Among other things, you'll find out how to:

- Secure reservations for the most sought after resorts and dates

- Manage your timeshare to get the most exchange value from it

- Get resort vacations for as little as $200 (for a week!)

- Multiply your timeshare use to provide as many vacations as you can schedule - the sky's the limit!

Owning timeshares can provide you with many benefits and years of wonderful vacations. Hopefully the insights and suggestions in this book will get you started on a good path, and soon **you'll be Winning the Timeshare Game**!

Acknowledgements and Credits

Image credits

All images are licensed under Creative Commons for Commercial Use.

Introduction: Start button - *Norlando Pobre*

Chapter 1, Winning the game:
  Game board - *Andy*

Chapter 2, Timeshare fundamentals:
  Schoolroom - *The shopping sherpa*
  Timeshare seasons: Leaf on snow - *Dawn Ellner*

Chapter 3, How THEY want you to buy a timeshare:
  Blank check - *RikkisRefuge Other*
  Driving me crazy - *Bark*
  Way out - *R/DV/RS*

Chapter 4, How YOU want to buy a timeshare:
  Coins - *Reza*

Chapter 5, Considerations before you buy a timeshare:
  Checklist - *StockMonkeys.com*

Chapter 6, Finances of buying a timeshare:
  Accounting - *o5com*

Chapter 7, How to research a timeshare bargain:
  Library books - *CCAC North Library*

Chapter 8, Case Studies - Researching timeshare
bargains:
    File folders - *Becky Wetherington*
    Vino Bello Resort - *Shell Vacations Hospitality*
    Kona Coast Resort - *Renee Viehmann*

Chapter 9, Putting it all together:
    Jigsaw puzzle - *skyfish81*
    Diving in - *Horia Varlan*

Chapter 10, Additional resources:
    Bookshelf - *Patrick Hoesly*

Acknowledgements and credits:
    Thank you - *Orin Zebest*

Cover: Maui beach, Sedona red rocks, and
    Game pieces - Deanna Keahey,
    Pool - Grand Velas Resort, Mexico

About the authors

Deanna Keahey has loved travel and adventure her whole life. She is a veteran of the travel industry, and for 7 years, ran an international tour company that operated trips in the US, Canada, Caribbean, Central and South America, and Europe. Her timeshare experiences began with one rather painful (but funny in hindsight) timeshare presentation years ago in Mexico. Since that time, she's enjoyed many fabulous timeshare vacations.

Brian Cook has owned timeshares for over a decade, owning at several different resorts. He has bought timeshares for as little as $1, and discovered many ins and outs of timeshare ownership. He's used every avenue available with his timeshares, learning to multiply his vacations and minimize the costs. He takes numerous timeshare trips each year, with 11 weeks of timeshare vacations in 2012.

When the two of them met, Brian showed Deanna how he uses timeshares to get many vacations and unbelievable deals. She quickly realized that Brian knew how to work the timeshare system much better than most people. Some people pay tens of thousands of dollars, and end up with a timeshare they barely use. Brian was paying a tiny amount for timeshares, and getting a huge amount of benefit from them.

Thus was born the idea for this project, **Winning the Timeshare Game**. Deanna wrote the book, while Brian provided insider information, practical tips, and a few of his personal success stories. We both hope that this information is useful for you, and that you get as much enjoyment out of timeshares as we do!